Copies

by Brad Slaight

Single copies of plays are sold for reading purposes only. The copying or duplicating of a play, or any part of play, by hand or by any other process, is an infringement of the copyright. Such infringement will be vigorously prosecuted

**Baker's Plays
7611 Sunset Blvd.
Los Angeles, CA 90042
BAKERSPLAYS.COM**

NOTICE

This book is offered for sale at the price quoted only on the understanding that, if any additional copies of the whole or any part are necessary for its production, such additional copies will be purchased. The attention of all purchasers is directed to the following: this work is fully protected under the copyright laws of the United States of America, the British Commonwealth, including Canada, and all other countries of the Copyright Union. Violations of the Copyright Law are punishable by fine or imprisonment, or both. The copying or duplication of this work or any part of this work, by hand or by any process, is an infringement of the copyright and will be vigorously prosecuted.

This play may not be produced by amateurs or professionals for public or private performance without first submitting application for performing rights. Royalties are due on all performances whether for charity or gain, or whether admission is charged or not. Since performance of this play without the payment of the royalty fee renders anybody participating liable to severe penalties imposed by the law, anybody acting in this play should be sure, before doing so, that the royalty fee has been paid. Professional rights, reading rights, radio broadcasting, television and all mechanical rights, etc. are strictly reserved. Application for performing rights should be made directly to BAKER'S PLAYS.

No one shall commit or authorize any act or omission by which the copyright of, or the right to copyright, this play may be impaired. No one shall make any changes in this play for the purpose of production.

Publication of this play does not imply availability for performance. Both amateurs and professionals considering a production are strongly advised in their own interest to apply to Baker's Plays for written permission before starting rehearsals, advertising, or booking a theatre.

Whenever the play is produced, the author's name must be carried in all publicity, advertising and programs. Also, the following notice must appear on all printed programs, "Produced by special arrangement with Baker's Plays."

Licensing fees for COPIES is based on a per performance rate and payable one week in advance of the production.

Please consult the Baker's Plays website at www.bakersplays.com or our current print catalogue for up to date licensing fee information.

Copyright © 2009 by Brad Slaight
Made in U.S.A.
All rights reserved.

COPIES
ISBN 978-0-87440-228-5
2031-B

COPIES was developed at the Young Conservatory of the American Conservatory Theater in San Francisco, California.

CHARACTERS

MICHAEL/ALLEN - a brand new teenage Copy (clone)
WENDY/MERRIS – female Copy; eats a lot
ZOOM/WARNER – not the brightest Copy in the cottage
BETTY/PETTY – a redesigned Copy
SANDRA/STEVENSON – a nice Copy who hopes for the best
MELISSA/PETROVICH – a Copy with an attitude and a mission
COUNSELOR SUE – an Original in charge of Cottage #4
AMY – an Original who comes to visit

SETTING

"Camp I.M.U." (Identical Memory Units) – an orientation camp for teenage clones.

If you want an elaborate set then go right ahead and build one, but the stage really doesn't need more than simple platforms and cubes to accommodate various settings.

TIME

The not too distant future

Scene One

*(**MICHAEL/ALLEN**, a 16-year-old newly made clone, stands in an isolated pool of light. He wears a bright colored industrial one-piece jumpsuit. Examines himself for a moment, as if for the first time. He looks at his hands and moves his fingers, enjoying the simplicity of being able to do that.)*

MICHAEL/ALLEN. The thing I remember the most is how "Me" just happened. Like somebody turning on a switch. The upload was so fast, so intense that I felt like I was about to explode. Billions of images coming at me in a nanosecond, swirling around in my mind and then planting themselves firmly in the fresh folds of my brain. A virtual and limitless eruption of people, places, events, and immediate memories that now belonged to me. All of a sudden I was alive. Fully aware. And my first ever thought was, "How lucky I am." Even luckier than my Original who took sixteen years to get to where I am from the very beginning. *(pause)* What a wonderful world I've been brought into…what a perfectly wonderful world!

Scene Two

(CAMP I.M.U.: Cottage #4 – Main Area. Lights up on four teenage clones ranging in age from 13 to 17: **WENDY/MERRIS, ZOOM/WARNER, BETTY/PETTY,** *and* **SANDRA/STEVENSON.** **WENDY** *and* **BETTY** *watch as* **ZOOM** *taps on the floor with the butt-end of a broom.* **SANDRA** *stands at the entrance keeping watch.)*

WENDY. That was a G.

ZOOM. What?

WENDY. You just spelled G-O-O-D instead of F-O-O-D.

ZOOM. No I didn't.

WENDY. You tapped seven times instead of six. Now she thinks we had "bad good" instead of "bad food."

BETTY. It wasn't too good it tasted like wood.

ZOOM. She'll know what I mean.

WENDY. Tell her you made a mistake.

ZOOM. Not worth it. Gimmee the next message?

BETTY. Mine would do fine.

*(***BETTY*** hands a note to* **ZOOM**. *He starts tapping on the floor.)*

ZOOM. A... *(taps once)* ...R... *(shoots a look to* **BETTY***; then taps eighteen times)* ...Come on, Betty, I thought I told you to lay off usin' so many letters at the end of the alphabet. I'm not gonna tap this.

WENDY. Melissa wants to hear it. Just do it.

ZOOM. You do it.

(He hands the broom to **WENDY**.*)*

SANDRA. Someone's coming.

*(***BETTY, ZOOM,*** and* **WENDY** *break up and assume relaxing positions on the stage.* **WENDY** *begins to mock-sweep the floor with the broom.* **COUNSELOR SUE** *enters, followed by* **MICHAEL/ALLEN**.*)*

COUNSELOR SUE. What's going on in here?

WENDY & SANDRA & ZOOM. Nothing.

COUNSELOR SUE. *(to MICHAEL/ALLEN)* This is Cottage #4. Your new home for…however long it takes.

(to others)

This is Allen.

ZOOM. Wow, he must be special…he's got a first name.

COUNSELOR SUE. Allen is the last name of his Original. But you knew that and just wanted to be a smart mouth.

(to MICHAEL/ALLEN)

You're rooming with Stevenson.

SANDRA. I'm Stevenson.

COUNSELOR SUE. First order of business for you is to read the rules. When you're done, read them again.

(COUNSELOR SUE hands MICHAEL/ALLEN a large book. She exits. They all take a moment to give MICHAEL/ALLEN a scrutinizing look.)

MICHAEL. Hi…I'm Allen. It is a pleasure to meet you all.

(He extends his hand. ZOOM, WENDY, and BETTY cross over to MICHAEL and ignore the hand. Instead they start to sniff him.)

ZOOM. Three days.

WENDY. No way, too strong. I'm saying a day. Maybe less.

ZOOM. Impossible.

WENDY. Not if he came from Mil-Tech.

BETTY. Mil-Tech? What the heck?

ZOOM. We never get a Mil-Techer.

(They all sniff some more.)

MICHAEL/ALLEN. What exactly…

WENDY. Sssh…don't say anything. You'll ruin the bet. This is the freshest I've ever smelled.

ZOOM. Three credits says he's at least two days.

WENDY. Covered. Sandra?

SANDRA. I'm not participating in this.

WENDY. Fine. Betty?

BETTY. A hundred days, is what I say.

SANDRA. Betty, that's just a dumb bet. You're going to lose.

WENDY. What do you care?

*(to **MICHAEL/ALLEN**)*

So what is it, Allen? How many days?

MICHAEL/ALLEN. How many days for what?

ZOOM. Since you were created, ya dumb Dolly.

MICHAEL/ALLEN. You mean my Point of Awareness?

WENDY. Whoa, someone got a special language upload.

ZOOM. One more thing his Original's gonna hate him for.

WENDY. So come on, Allen…when were you made? You know, in the lab.

MICHAEL/ALLEN. My official Point of Awareness was 22 hours and 7 minutes ago.

WENDY. Woo-hoo. I win.

ZOOM. Dumb luck.

WENDY. So you were made by Mil-Tech?

MICHAEL/ALLEN. Sun Labs.

BETTY. Son of a gun, he's made by Sun!

SANDRA. That's the trendy new place they were telling us about.

*(They all move away from **MICHAEL/ALLEN** and cross back over to the area they were at before. **WENDY** takes the broom and is about to resume tapping on the floor. Looks at her watch and decides not to.)*

WENDY. We'd better stop.

ZOOM. We still got 10 minutes.

WENDY. They might come early. Better safe than sorry. We don't want to get Melissa in more trouble than she's already in.

*(**MICHAEL/ALLEN** crosses over to them.)*

MICHAEL/ALLEN. Who is Melissa?

SANDRA. Melissa is one of us.

MICHAEL/ALLEN. Does she live under the floor?

ZOOM. *(to MICHAEL/ALLEN)* Dumb Dolly.

SANDRA. No, she lives here…but for right now she's in a room underneath us. So we tap messages to keep her company.

MICHAEL/ALLEN. You tap messages with a broom? That seems rather archaic.

SANDRA. That's exactly why it works.

(**ZOOM** *shakes his head and crosses to a platform and sits.* **WENDY** *retrieves a bag of tortilla chips, devours them.*)

SANDRA. *(to MICHAEL/ALLEN)* So what's your name?

ZOOM. Bet he doesn't have one.

MICHAEL/ALLEN. I have a name. It's Allen.

ZOOM. She don't mean your Original's name, fresh flesh.

BETTY. Fresh flesh!

SANDRA. What name do you call yourself?

MICHAEL/ALLEN. Allen.

WENDY. Yeah, he definitely just fell off the Petri dish.

SANDRA. You need a first name.

MICHAEL/ALLEN. They said the Originals endow us with our first names.

SANDRA. That's something that will happen later. For right now why don't you pick a first name for yourself that we can call you.

MICHAEL/ALLEN. *(thinks for a moment)* Allen is fine.

WENDY. Allen Allen?

(**ZOOM** *crosses to him.*)

ZOOM. Well, it ain't fine with us. Pick a first name or I'll give you one. And you're not gonna like the one I give you.

SANDRA. Back off, Zoom…you had the same problem when you first got here.

WENDY. Yeah, and it took you three days to come up with "Zoom."

ZOOM. Two days.

MICHAEL/ALLEN. When did you arrive here?

ZOOM. Three months and twelve days ago.

BETTY. It hasn't been great, but I've been here for eight.

SANDRA. She means eight months. I've been here for 5 months 3 days.

WENDY. 6 months 13 days…and Melissa's got the record with 10 months 22 days.

MICHAEL/ALLEN. That is a long period of time to spend at an orientation camp.

WENDY. Don't tell me you really bought their line about a quick turnaround. They only tell you that to get you here without melting down.

MICHAEL/ALLEN. They promised I'd meet my Original during the first week.

SANDRA. You might. But that doesn't mean you'll go home with him right away.

WENDY. I can't remember ever hearing about anybody going home after the first meeting.

SANDRA. I think there have been a few.

WENDY. Not in a long time.

SANDRA. Maybe he'll be different.

ZOOM. Yeah, right.

BETTY. Your first reception could make you an exception.

ZOOM. Hey, Sandra…you just had a meeting with your Original last week. Why don't you tell him how that went?

SANDRA. That has nothing to do with him.

WENDY. It'll give him an idea of what to expect.

MICHAEL/ALLEN. *(to **SANDRA**)* You met with your Original? That's exciting!

ZOOM. Yeah…for the *third* time.

SANDRA. My Original's parents are just being careful, that's all. It was their decision…

WENDY. Careful? They're paranoid. It's not like you're getting married to their little precious or anything.

SANDRA. But I will be living with them and spending a lot of time with Charlene so they just want to be sure we get along well.

BETTY. It would be wrong if they don't get along.

ZOOM. 'How you gonna get along? Charlene's evil.

SANDRA. No she's not.

WENDY. You're the one that told us that, Sandra.

SANDRA. I was angry. She's really not that bad.

WENDY. She treats you like a fool, expecting you to do tricks for her and keep her laughing. You know she's just going to abuse you if you ever do go home with her.

SANDRA. I think we can work this out. Next time I meet with her…we'll hit it off better and I'll be on my way out of here.

MICHAEL/ALLEN. I'm sure you will. You can make it work.

SANDRA. Thank you.

ZOOM. Ah, what does he know? Mr. Day-old-no-name.

BETTY. Wendy may face that sorrow, when she meets hers tomorrow.

ZOOM. Yeah, that's right…Wendy's gonna meet with her Original again tomorrow.

MICHAEL/ALLEN. That's exciting.

(**WENDY** *crosses to the bag and grabs a packaged cupcake, opens it.*)

ZOOM. It's not gonna happen.

SANDRA. Wendy's gained fifteen pounds since the last time.

WENDY. Seventeen as of this morning.

SANDRA. Congratulations!

MICHAEL/ALLEN. Is it good to have a significant weight gain?

SANDRA. For her it is. Wendy's Original has a bit of a weight problem.

WENDY. A bit? If Carla was any bigger, she'd moo.

(**ZOOM** *and* **BETTY** *laugh.*)

MICHAEL/ALLEN. Should you really be talking about your Original like that?

WENDY. She can't hear me.

SANDRA. We have a pact here, Allen. Everything said in Cottage #4, stays in Cottage #4. It's like Las Vegas... without all the gambling and fun stuff.

WENDY. And that means not telling the Counselors.

ZOOM. Yeah, so don't get any stupid ideas.

MICHAEL/ALLEN. If that is the protocol here I will not say anything. I just don't think we should speak so poorly about someone who is the very reason we exist.

ZOOM. She's just sayin' the truth. Her Original's been supersized!

BETTY. There once was a teen from the lab
Who was created and put on a slab
She woke up and said
I'd rather be dead
Then to have my Original's flab!

WENDY. Majestic, Betty!

ZOOM. Nice!

WENDY. That's the first time you've ever done a limerick.

*(**BETTY** enjoys all the new attention being paid her. **SANDRA** crosses over to **MICHAEL/ALLEN**.)*

SANDRA. How about "Michael" for your name to use here? You look like a Michael.

WENDY. Let him pick his own name.

SANDRA. It's just a suggestion...

MICHAEL/ALLEN. I guess if I need another name, Michael is as good as any. After I join my Original, I'll let him change it to whatever he prefers.

SANDRA. Okay, Michael. I'm Sandra...that's Wendy... Betty...Zoom...and there's one more who stays here... the one we were talking about...her name is Melissa.

WENDY. Melissa is the best.

ZOOM. Melissa's the number one.

BETTY. She's better than great, Melissa's always first rate.

SANDRA. If she's so great then why does she spend more time in isolation than here?

MICHAEL. Isolation?

WENDY. That's right…the big "I." That's how they keep us in line here. One wrong move and you'll be down there, too. All alone.

SANDRA. You're scaring him, Wendy.

WENDY. He should be scared. Scared right out of his stem cells scared. So he'll do everything he can to avoid it.

BETTY. Isolation is no vacation.

MICHAEL. Clones should never be isolated. It can have a severe psychological effect on us. We're not designed to be alone.

(ZOOM moves in on him in a threatening manner.)

ZOOM. Don't you ever use that word in here again!

MICHAEL. Isolated?

WENDY. The C to the L to the O to the N to the E word.

SANDRA. We don't call ourselves that, Michael. We prefer "Copy."

MICHAEL. Copy? That's a better word than clone?

ZOOM. I told you not to use that word.

(He makes a threatening move towards MICHAEL. SANDRA jumps between them.)

SANDRA. *(to ZOOM)* Give him some time to get used to it. He just got here.

(to MICHAEL)

We think "Copy" is a better word. The Counselors never call us that, but when we're together we do.

WENDY. You won't find that in the rulebook.

BETTY. Rules are for fools.

WENDY. Hey, I got an idea…after nutrition let's tell Melissa about Michael. That will give her plenty of time to think about how she wants to initiate him.

ZOOM. Oh, yeah…now that's somethin' to look forward to.
MICHAEL. *(worried)* What do you mean by "initiation"?
ZOOM. More than that…a Meliss-initiation!

(**WENDY** *and* **ZOOM** *share an evil laugh.*)

WENDY. My favorite thing of all…a Meliss-initiation!
ZOOM. *(to* **MICHAEL***)* She don't like new Copies like you. 'specially ones that come from some snooty designer lab.
MICHAEL. I'm sure once Melissa and I have an opportunity to talk we will become very good friends.
WENDY. Hold onto that dream.

(*An electronic buzzer is heard.*)

MICHAEL. What's that?
SANDRA. Midday nutrition time.

(**ZOOM**, **WENDY**, *and* **BETTY** *start to exit. As they pass* **MICHAEL**…)

ZOOM. You just wait. When Melissa comes back here you're gonna be initiated. And there's nothin' you can do about it.
BETTY. The worst thing in the nation is a Meliss-initiation.

(**WENDY** *and* **ZOOM** *exit.* **BETTY** *follows after them.*)

SANDRA. Don't worry about it. Let's go eat.

(**SANDRA** *takes a concerned* **MICHAEL** *by the arm and leads him off.*)

Scene Three

*(Isolation Area. A light on **MELISSA**. She stands in front of a bright red chair and is talking out loud as if giving a speech.)*

MELISSA. ...But it takes all of you to make this thing work. By ourselves we're nothing, we can't be heard. But together we are one loud voice that cannot be ignored. Together we will shake the very foundation of what they think is right, and what we know is wrong! And we...

*(She stops in reaction to the sound of a deadbolt being undone; quickly sits down in the chair. **COUNSELOR SUE** enters.)*

COUNSELOR SUE. Who you talking to Petrovich?

MELISSA. No one.

COUNSELOR SUE. Sure sounded like someone. Maybe the solitude is getting to you. You melting down on us?

MELISSA. Not at all.

*(**COUNSELOR SUE** looks around the room.)*

COUNSELOR SUE. They told me you had the viewing screen on just one time...and that was for only 5 minutes.

MELISSA. All that educational stuff they show gives me a headache. If they showed Wrestlemania I'd watch it.

COUNSELOR SUE. Your smart mouth isn't making things any better for you.

MELISSA. It's just an observation.

COUNSELOR SUE. Most clones prefer watching the screen to sitting alone with nothing to look at or any kind of sensory input.

MELISSA. Most clones are weak.

COUNSELOR SUE. Well, there's no rule that says you have to watch it. Although it wouldn't hurt to work your brain muscle.

MELISSA. I have a great imagination. I can be anywhere I want to be just by thinking about it.

COUNSELOR SUE. So you've been using your Original's memories? That's good.

MELISSA. Her memories are boring. I've been using my own.

COUNSELOR SUE. You don't have any yet.

MELISSA. Not memories, thoughts…and my thoughts are to the future.

(**COUNSELOR SUE** *looks around the room.*)

COUNSELOR SUE. They also tell me you've been talking to yourself a lot. Don't deny it because I heard you before I came in here.

MELISSA. Okay, sometimes. For smirks. I'm the most interesting person I know.

(**COUNSELOR SUE** *bristles at that.*)

COUNSELOR SUE. You're not allowed to refer to yourself as a person! You are a clone. That's page one of the Rulebook and you know it.

(**MELISSA** *is stung by that.*)

MELISSA. So I talk to myself. Big deal. It's just a time-killer.

COUNSELOR SUE. Talking to oneself is a sign of mental instability.

MELISSA. Mental stability is highly overrated.

COUNSELOR SUE. And sarcasm is a sign of insecurity. You don't fool me, Petrovich. To the others in your cottage you're some kind of rebel who speaks her own mind. But I can see the fear on your face…in your eyes.

(*She looks hard at* **MELISSA**, *who looks away from her.*)

COUNSELOR SUE. Here's something for you to think about during the rest of the time you're down here. You have a meeting with your Original in two weeks.

MELISSA. *(concerned)* Already? I thought they wanted to wait another month.

COUNSELOR SUE. They're very unhappy with your progress. They're getting impatient. And let me tell you something…it has to go well this time. You better find a way to show them your attitude has changed. To show them you are what they want.

MELISSA. I'll never be what they want.

COUNSELOR SUE. I'm sure you won't. But they told me something that might motivate you. They said that if you don't show positive improvement this time…they will move to have you redesigned.

*(This hits **MELISSA** hard.)*

COUNSELOR SUE. Personally, I think they should have done that a long time ago…because you're a lost cause.

*(**COUNSELOR SUE** exits.)*

Scene Four

(Cottage #4 – Bunk Area #2. Night. Sometime around 2200 hours. In the darkness we hear a **MAN'S VOICE** *over a loudspeaker.)*

MAN'S VOICE *(V.O.)* Attention all clones...we are pleased to report this Breaking News. Today, resident Roth and resident Kelsey successfully completed their orientation requirements and have left Camp I.M.U. on their way to join their Originals. Sweet dreams.

(We hear the sound of canned applause. Lights up on stage left revealing **WENDY**, **ZOOM** *and* **BETTY** *in a cramped sleeping area of the cottage.)*

ZOOM. Yeah, but how many more have loaded in here.

WENDY. Out of this whole camp only two are getting out this week?

BETTY. Wendy will make three.

ZOOM. Don't count on it.

WENDY. Come on, Zoom. I got a good feeling. Last time it almost happened but I was too thin. With the extra weight I put on...I'm sure she'll take me home.

ZOOM. You know better'n to get your hopes up.

WENDY. I'm not saying my hopes are up, just that I have a feeling.

BETTY. It's oh so healing to have a good feeling.

ZOOM. Betty, can't you stay in your own room for one night?

WENDY. Melissa's not back yet. She'd be all alone.

ZOOM. She could go stay with Sandra and Michael.

WENDY. Their place is even smaller than this one.

ZOOM. Just stay outta my way, Betty. You're startin' to bug me.

*(***BETTY*** is angered by that and tries to tell him off, but all that comes out is...)*

BETTY. Betty, Betty, spaghetti!

ZOOM. And when you're tired your rhymin' skills are really lame.

(**BETTY** *moves a few more inches away from him.*)

ZOOM. *(to* **WENDY***)* So whatta you think of the new guy Michael?

WENDY. I try not to.

ZOOM. Melissa is gonna have a carnival with that boy.

WENDY. Yeah, if she ever gets out. This is the longest they've ever kept her in there.

ZOOM. She'll be all right. She's Melissa. And she's gonna microwave Michael when she comes back.

WENDY. She does hate overly positive Copies like him.

BETTY. I like Mike.

ZOOM. You would.

WENDY. There's definitely something about him that's different from most of the Copies in this place.

ZOOM. Well, that's not gonna matter to Melissa. She'll bust him good.

WENDY. Too bad I won't be here to see if she does or not.

ZOOM. Whatta you mean?

WENDY. I'll be on my way home with Carla before she gets out.

ZOOM. Yeah, right.

(*Lights cross-fade to stage right on* **SANDRA** *and* **MICHAEL**.)

Scene Five

(Cottage #4 – Bunk Area #3. Same time as Scene 4. **MICHAEL** *is sitting on his bunk and speaks into a small handheld device.* **SANDRA** *is nearby on her bunk.)*

MICHAEL. It's my first night at Camp I.M.U and things are going exceedingly well. The others in my cottage are all really great. Our sleeping quarters are really nice, but a little small. Actually the room I share with someone is about the size of your closet. Counselor Sue told me these rooms were built for just one occupant but they had to double-up due to demand. Well, that's all for now…can't wait to meet you. Hope it's real soon.

(He places the device on top of his backpack.)

MICHAEL. Should I change the part about this place being small?

SANDRA. Why? It is small.

MICHAEL. I don't want to make him think I am complaining. Nobody likes a complaining Clone…I mean Copy.

SANDRA. He's not going to hear it anyway. We're not allowed to communicate with our Originals while we're here unless they come to see us. It's the old "seen and not heard" thing.

MICHAEL. I know…I read the rulebook.

SANDRA. You did? The whole thing?

MICHAEL. Yes.

SANDRA. You're the first one to ever do that.

MICHAEL. I'm keeping an audio journal of my thoughts here. I'll play it for Robert later after we're together. He'll want to know about my time here…won't he?

SANDRA. Hard to say. I know mine wouldn't. But she's… well…she's different.

*(**MICHAEL** looks at a drawing on the wall.)*

MICHAEL. Did you draw that illustration on the wall?

SANDRA. That was Richter…the guy right before you. He had a thing about dinosaurs.

MICHAEL. Oh, that's what they are. I thought they were cows.

SANDRA. No, you see that one…that's supposed to be a T-Rex. He's chasing the others. Counselor Sue said she'd have someone paint over it, but I'm not holding my breath.

MICHAEL. What was Richter like?

SANDRA. Richter was really strange. We all think something went wrong in the lab. That boy just wasn't right.

MICHAEL. So he got to go home with his Original. Good for him, huh?

SANDRA. Well, not really. He had some problems. He had to be…

MICHAEL. Redesigned?

SANDRA. Worse.

MICHAEL. Harvested?

SANDRA. Uh…yeah.

(beat)

Betty was redesigned.

MICHAEL. I wondered about her. The fact that she rhymes everything is very odd.

SANDRA. She's only been like that for a few weeks. She used to be very well spoken. Her Original didn't like that. Wanted her to be more "fun"…so they redesigned her to speak like a nursery rhyme.

MICHAEL. Well, if that's what her Original wanted then it's a good thing…right?

SANDRA. Some might say that. But Betty isn't one of them. Sometimes I can tell she's really frustrated. Like part of her old self is still inside trying desperately to get out.

(The lights start to dim.)

MICHAEL. 2200 already?

SANDRA. Best time of the day as far as I'm concerned. I love dreaming. That's the great part about being a Copy… every dream is brand new. Like a movie we're seeing for the first time.

MICHAEL. It's not going to be easy to recharge tonight… not with my adrenaline levels running so high right now.

SANDRA. Well, try. Tomorrow we have classes all day and the Counselors are always harder the first day of the week.

*(**SANDRA** rolls over to go to sleep. **MICHAEL** picks his recorder back up and whispers into it…)*

MICHAEL. Bedtime around here is at 2200 hours…I mean ten o'clock. I have to go to classes tomorrow, just like you do. This is really great training.

(His forced smile quickly fades, along with the lights.)

Scene Six

(Cottage #4 – Main Area. The next day. **WENDY** *sits with a scowl and a big bag full of junk food.* **BETTY** *opens a box of donuts and hands one to* **WENDY**, *she begins to eat it but it's obvious she doesn't enjoy it.* **MICHAEL**, **SANDRA**, *and* **ZOOM** *enter. They spot* **WENDY**.*)*

SANDRA. Oh no...Wendy.

BETTY. Yes, my dear, poor Wendy is still here.

SANDRA. I really thought she'd take you home this time.

WENDY. Me too.

ZOOM. What happened?

*(***WENDY*** talks while she continues to eat.)*

WENDY. A broken leg?

SANDRA. What?

WENDY. Carla broke her leg.

SANDRA. So she didn't make it?

WENDY. Oh, she made it...all *200* lbs. of her! She says she's only 180 but the metal chair she sat in was groaning the entire time. She's huge. She broke her leg right at the start of summer, so while all the other kids were out swimming and biking and running around she sat home and wore out the refrigerator. She said it's not her fault...but I don't think anyone force-fed her that carbapalooza.

SANDRA. So that extra weight you've put on wasn't enough?

WENDY. Not even close.

MICHAEL. There's always a possibility that she might lose it when her leg heals.

WENDY. Doubt it. She's been out of the cast for two weeks now and is complete denial. There's no way she's going to go anywhere but up. And she made it very clear that I'm no good to her unless I look exactly like her. She was pissed that I didn't. Like I'm a mind reader or something. She told me she had all these plans for me to fill in for her and now she'll have to wait. It's all my fault, she tells me.

ZOOM. Ain't that just like an Original to blame the Copy for their problems.

SANDRA. Well…then you'll just have to work harder at eating more.

(**SANDRA** *crosses to her and pulls a box of licorice from the bag.*)

SANDRA. You have to put on more weight and we'll all help you…

BETTY. I'll load you up with calories…or my name isn't…

(desperate for a rhyme; painful to her)

…Mallory.

ZOOM. You're name ain't Mallory.

BETTY. You see, that's not me!

WENDY. There's no way I can gain all that weight.

SANDRA. Sure you can. You're her Copy. Whatever she can do, you certainly can do.

MICHAEL. Actually it doesn't work that way. Genetically you may both be predisposed to weight gain, but there are other factors at play such as metabolism, activity levels, personal discipline….

(They all glare at **MICHAEL**. *He stops.)*

ZOOM. Mute it, Copy.

MICHAEL. No, I mean…it's just that our bodies are made from the Original's DNA but some things like metabolism aren't always going to be identical. They're working on that though.

ZOOM. And you know this because?

WENDY. Because he has a genius IQ, that's why. I saw his file.

SANDRA. How did you see his file?

WENDY. Counselor Sue made the mistake of trusting Betty and I alone in her office for ten minutes.

BETTY. She took a break, big mistake.

ZOOM. So how smart is he?

WENDY. 179.

ZOOM. Day-um.

SANDRA. That's great, Michael. You're a whiz kid.

MICHAEL. That's not great at all. It's 65 points higher than my Original's IQ.

ZOOM. How do you know?

MICHAEL. Because they left me alone for a few minutes at the lab. I opened my file on the computer.

SANDRA. You were alone?

MICHAEL. Well, not really. There was a Prefab in the room with me. She still had a few hours to cook so she wasn't aware yet.

WENDY. So you broke the rules before you were even out of the lab.

ZOOM. Whattaya know…he's not so pure after all. Nice!

BETTY. It's your time, might as well do the crime.

MICHAEL. I never should have been this intelligent. They are supposed to make us a slightly smarter in order to assist with homework, but they tweaked me a little too high.

ZOOM. So you're a Malform?

MICHAEL. I'm not a Malform.

ZOOM. Malform, Malform!

WENDY. Mute it, Zoom. Or I'll tell him your IQ.

*(That quiets **ZOOM**.)*

ZOOM. It's low because they made me to help my Original be better at sports.

VOICE. Yeah, Zoom's a halfback with a half-brain.

*(They all turn to see **MELISSA**.)*

ZOOM & WENDY. Melissa!

BETTY. Melissa, we missed-ya.

*(Everyone except **MICHAEL** runs to **MELISSA**, hugs mixed with high fives.)*

MELISSA. Easy…I've only been gone three days.

SANDRA. That's a long time, especially to be alone.

WENDY. I think I'd die if I was alone that long.

ZOOM. And that's what makes Melissa better'n all of us. She can take it.

MELISSA. That's right…I took it and I took it good. An hour didn't go by when they didn't try to offer me an early out. You see they knew the punishment they gave me was too harsh, but instead of just letting me out they tried to make some kind of a deal. "Admit you were wrong and we'll let you out." No way. "Promise that you'll be a good little Copy from now on and you're free to go." Not promising you anything.

ZOOM. Melissa's tough.

WENDY. And a martyr for the cause.

BETTY. She's smarter than a martyr.

MELISSA. Well said, Mother Goose. I am smarter. They'll think twice next time about how long they put Melissa in isolation.

MICHAEL. You could avoid the next time by just behaving.

(MELISSA's eyes dilate; she pushes the others out of the way to expose MICHAEL.)

MELISSA. Who is that poor excuse for recombined DNA?

ZOOM. That's the new guy I was tappin' to you about.

MELISSA. That's "M" huh?

WENDY. Stands for Michael.

ZOOM. But he didn't come up with that name. Sandra gave it to him. He wanted to wait for his Original to do it.

MELISSA. Well how totally and utterly subservient of him.

(MELISSA walks over to MICHAEL and sniffs him.)

SANDRA. Melissa, he doesn't know any better. Don't hurt him.

ZOOM. Shut up, Sandra.

(to MELISSA)

Hurt him.

MELISSA. *(to* **MICHAEL***)* You don't even know me, but you dare to take a shot at me?

MICHAEL. I didn't mean to offend you…it was just logical advice.

MELISSA. Advice?

MICHAEL. Yes, from what I gather you have gotten in more than your share of trouble here and spent way too much time in isolation.

MELISSA. So?

MICHAEL. Therefore, I was just suggesting that you behave yourself and you would never be sent there again.

MELISSA. Well aren't you the little genius.

WENDY. Actually we found out that he is…179 IQ.

*(**MELISSA** is impressed with that, but hides it.)*

MELISSA. *(to* **MICHAEL***)* Look, I don't need anybody to tell me how to act. I think for myself and I watch out for myself. You got that?

MICHAEL. Uh…yes…in the future I will not offer any advice to you about…you.

MELISSA. Better not.

*(**MELISSA** walks away from **MICHAEL**.)*

ZOOM. You mean you're not going to pound him? I was lookin' forward to it.

*(**MELISSA** crosses to **ZOOM**.)*

MELISSA. If you're in such a hurry to see pounding, maybe I can just cut out the middleman and total you.

ZOOM. No…I was just…

MELISSA. Just being a Dolly again, right?

ZOOM. Right, I was being a Dolly.

WENDY. Are you at least going to give him a Meliss-initiation?

ZOOM. Yeah, make it a good one!

*(**MELISSA** thinks for a moment.)*

MELISSA. Bring him front and center.

(ZOOM and WENDY grab MICHAEL and drag him to MELISSA and then back away, leaving the two of them alone.)

ZOOM. How about "Walk the Worm"?

WENDY. No, do "Spank-a-sonic."

ZOOM. "Boston Beartrap."

WENDY. That's lame. How about "Rock, Paper, Blisters"?

SANDRA. Last time we did that someone got hurt.

ZOOM. Yeah, that someone was me.

WENDY. I know… "The Grand Canyon Two-Step"!

BETTY. Over and under, you blunder then wonder!

WENDY. Yeah, "The Grand Canyon Two-Step"…how about it, Melissa?

(ZOOM, WENDY, and BETTY ad lib their excitement about it, while SANDRA protests. MELISSA holds up her hand to silence them.)

MELISSA. I've made my decision…

BETTY. …with Melissa precision.

MELISSA. "Search the Purge!"

ZOOM. All right, "Search the Purge"…uh…What's that?

WENDY. Must have been even before my time.

MELISSA. It's a new one. I just thought of it. Perfect for this boy wonder.

ZOOM. How does it work?

MELISSA. Form a line here.

(ZOOM, WENDY, SANDRA and BETTY line up like soldiers, facing out to the audience.)

MELISSA. We all know that when we were made the Creators purposely left out one important human trait… the urge for sex. That's why they can stick us in here together. Boy teens and girl teens, all living and sleeping under the same roof, day in and day out. They can't do that with Original teens. They'd all be jumping and bumping and humping in no time. Gotta split them up. Gotta separate them. Gotta have chaperones. They all got "the urge."

ZOOM & WENDY. …the URGE!

BETTY. Our urge has been purged.

MELISSA. Yanked right out of us. Neutralized, neutered, and nowhere to be found.

ZOOM & WENDY. Nowhere to be found.

MELISSA. While Originals live for it, it's dead in us. While Originals fight for it, we're never going to see the front lines. While Originals are driven by it, our sex drive is in park. The urge.

ZOOM & WENDY. …the URGE!

BETTY. A surge that they purged.

MELISSA. But I'm thinking, maybe they didn't get it all. Maybe down deep, hiding behind some confused chromosomes, a little residual of the urge hangs on that lived through the purge. One speck of romance exists in us all. Lying dormant, waiting for the day it can surface and scream out loud to us, "you are a bumping, grinding love program just like everyone else. The Originals got nothing on you!"

MICHAEL. But it would be a disaster if we had the urge.

MELISSA. No, it would only be a disaster if we produced offspring. I don't think any of us wants to see a Copy from a Copy. But there's no reason why we shouldn't at least have the ability to enjoy the urge.

BETTY. No merging, just urging.

*(**MELISSA** gets real close to **MICHAEL**. Looks deep into his eyes. The she grabs his head and opens his mouth, looking down into his throat.)*

MELISSA. Is the urge somewhere hiding down there, Michael? Does your 179 IQ make your engine run hot? Do you feel more than the rest of us? Come out, come out, wherever you urge!

(She looks for a moment and then closes his mouth.)

So here's how we play "Search the Urge." You will have to kiss each one of us and then we will see if it has any affect on you.

WENDY. Kiss us?

SANDRA. Really?

MELISSA. Everyone except Zoom.

ZOOM. Good.

MELISSA. You don't get off that easy. You and I are going to kiss to show him how it's done.

ZOOM. I don't know how it's done.

(**MELISSA** *crosses to him.*)

MELISSA. I'm pretty sure it works like this.

(*She grabs* **ZOOM** *and plants an awkward kiss on his lips.*)

ZOOM. That's a kiss?

MELISSA. You've seen it in movies they show us on movie night.

ZOOM. I always thought they were just talkin' really really close.

MELISSA. Nope, it's kissing. It's supposedly the first sign of the urge. You don't even want to know where it goes from there.

SANDRA. I know what it leads to…or at least have the memory from when my Original did it.

(*They all look at* **SANDRA** *for a moment.*)

MELISSA. Okay, Michael…it's your turn now. You're going to kiss Sandra, then Wendy, then Betty and then me.

MICHAEL. I have no desire to do that.

ZOOM. You don't got a choice…it's your initiation.

WENDY. We all had to be initiated…now it's your turn.

BETTY. You've earned a turn.

MICHAEL. What if I refuse?

MELISSA. Then I'll hurt you. Do you think your Original is going to want you if you're all bruised up like a bad peach?

(**MICHAEL** *thinks about it for a moment.*)

MICHAEL. Can't I do the "Grand Canyon Two-Step" instead?

MELISSA. You don't even know what that is?

MICHAEL. Anything's better than having to kiss someone.

MELISSA. That's just something they planted in you. So you wouldn't want to. It's a reflex. If anyone can overcome it, you can.

(**MICHAEL** *reluctantly crosses over to* **SANDRA**. *She puckers up for him and he leans in to her and presses his lips against hers. They both react like they just tasted bad milk.*)

SANDRA. Sorry Michael.

(**MICHAEL** *crosses to* **WENDY** *who isn't all that excited about this either. He closes in for a kiss and the kiss lasts much longer than when he kissed* **SANDRA**.)

MELISSA. Now we're onto something. You liked that right?

MICHAEL. *(licking his lips)* Not her, the chocolate on her lips.

(**MICHAEL** *crosses to* **BETTY** *who puckers up*)

BETTY. Betty is ready.

(**MICHAEL** *kisses her quickly. Nothing. Wants to be done with this.*)

MELISSA. Now me.

MICHAEL. This isn't working. I don't feel anything. They don't feel anything.

(**MELISSA** *crosses to* **MICHAEL** *and initiates a kiss. She forces him to stay lip-locked to her for as long as possible. He fights it all the way. Finally she lets him go.*)

WENDY. Wow!

SANDRA. Well, if any urge was hiding in there…that sure would have put a spotlight on it.

MELISSA. Michael?

MICHAEL. Oh…uh…Nothing.

(**MELISSA** *looks at him for a moment.*)

MELISSA. Yeah, me neither.

(**MELISSA** *sulks away from them and sits down.*)

WENDY. Is that it?

ZOOM. The initiation is over?

MELISSA. Yup.

ZOOM. But no one got hurt.

BETTY. We weren't even on the verge of finding an urge.

(*They all look pretty rejected.*)

MICHAEL. So I'm initiated, right?

WENDY. Looks like it.

MELISSA. Yeah, you're one of us now. Like that's a big thing.

MICHAEL. Somehow I pictured some sort of celebration afterwards.

(**WENDY** *reaches in her bag and pulls something out.*)

WENDY. Here…have a party.

(*She tosses him a donut.*)

Scene Seven

(Another day. A camp classroom. **BETTY, WENDY, ZOOM, MELISSA, SANDRA** *and* **MICHAEL** *sit in folding chairs.* **COUNSELOR SUE** *leads them in verbal drills.)*

GROUP.
"A big black bug bit a big black bear, made the big black bear bleed blood."

COUNSELOR SUE. Again…

GROUP.
"A big black bug bit a big black bear, made the big black bear bleed blood."

COUNSELOR SUE. Solos…Stevenson.

SANDRA. "Six thick thistle sticks."

COUNSELOR SUE. Merris…

WENDY. "She sells sea shells by the sea shore."

COUNSELOR SUE. Warner…

ZOOM. *(struggles)* "Fat frogs…frying…uh…flying…past…flast…fast."

COUNSELOR SUE. Wrong! Do it again!

ZOOM. "Fat frogs flying past fast."

COUNSELOR SUE. Better. Petrovich…

MELISSA. Tongue twisters are for twits.

COUNSELOR SUE. Not sanctioned! Do one from the book!

MELISSA. *(bored with it all)* "Rubber baby buggy bumpers."

COUNSELOR SUE. Petty…

ZOOM. Like she needs the practice.

BETTY. *(excited)* "He ran from the Indies to the Andes in his undies! He ran from the Indies to the Andes in his undies!" "He ran…

COUNSELOR SUE. Stop. Once was enough, Petty. Allen.

MICHAEL. "Sneezing with wheezing is easy if sneezing is pleasing. Easing the wheezing gives meaning to sneezing."

COUNSELOR SUE. Very good…but I've never heard that before.

MICHAEL. That's because I wrote it.

ZOOM. Not sanctioned.

COUNSELOR SUE. I'll allow it.

(beat)

Now that our tongues have had a workout it's time to move on to the brain.

(**MICHAEL** *watches the others as they shift in their seats, bracing themselves for the onslaught of questions.*)

COUNSELOR SUE. Stevenson…89 times 56…

SANDRA. 4,984

COUNSELOR SUE. Correct. Merris…589 minus 175…

WENDY. 414

COUNSELOR SUE. Correct. Warner…168 divided by 12…

ZOOM. Uh…it's…

COUNSELOR SUE. Quickly!

ZOOM. 16.

COUNSELOR SUE. Wrong…wrong! It's 14! You got it wrong. That can't happen.

ZOOM. Hey I was close.

COUNSELOR SUE. Close is not good enough. The most powerful tool you possess on your way to becoming a well functioning clone is your brain and the ability to use it quickly. You must always keep it sharp because you'll never know when your Original will need you to take a test for them, or figure out a solution to one of their problems, or just act as their own personal filing system.

MELISSA. That's 'cause they're too lazy to do it themselves.

COUNSELOR SUE. Don't start, not today.

ZOOM. Yeah…they're just lazy.

(**COUNSELOR SUE** *crosses over to* **ZOOM.**)

COUNSELOR SUE. Oh really? Well, let remind you…clones don't get to have an opinion. That's not why you were created. Nobody wants to hear what a clone thinks... especially YOU.

(**ZOOM** *looks around at the others, more hurt than angry.*)

COUNSELOR SUE. Oh, are you upset, Warner? You going to cry?

ZOOM. I'm not gonna cry...

COUNSELOR SUE. Well you better not because nobody wants a crying clone. And you better get used to having mean things said to you because in the real world you're going to get a lot harsher treatment than what I give you here. And let me tell you...let me tell you all...clones are not allowed to cry. Ever. No matter how you're treated. No matter what is said to you.

(*to* **ZOOM**)

If you cry in the real world you'll be redesigned so fast your chromosomes will spin.

(*looks around the room at the others*)

You all think I'm being cruel, don't you? Let me tell you something. I'm an angel compared to what you might encounter out there. You will be poked, laughed at, ridiculed, used, abused and ignored. You were created for one purpose: To be useful.

MELISSA. That's not the main purpose...

(**COUNSELOR SUE** *is on her quickly.*)

COUNSELOR SUE. Not another word, Petrovich...or you'll be in isolation for a week!

(**MELISSA** *backs down.* **COUNSELOR SUE** *continues her speech to the others.*)

Oh, sure there's always a remote chance that you'll end up in a family that will treat you like one of their own. But don't count on it. When you leave this place, it will be to serve your Original however they want you to serve. The only hope you have to survive in the world of the Originals is to be fast and smart.

WENDY. Warner was designed to be athletic, not smart. He's a jock.

COUNSELOR SUE. Doesn't matter. He may need to be someday and you're all here to train for any and all potential services.

(pause)

Now let's try it again, Warner…85 times 15…

ZOOM. *(angry)* 1275.

COUNSELOR SUE. Correct.

(to all)

It's about focus. All of you were designed to one degree or another to problem-solve. To think quickly and accurately. But there's no room for daydreams and wandering minds. My job is to prepare all of you for the real world. But clones like you make it very hard for me to do my job.

*(**COUNSELOR SUE** crosses back to the front of the classroom.)*

COUNSELOR SUE. Looks like we have just enough time left today for "recall."

(There is a bit of a groan from the Copies.)

COUNSELOR SUE. *(to **MICHAEL**)* Allen, this is a drill that puts you in touch with the memories that were implanted in you. It's good to recall specific moments from your Original's life. They are in you already, but the closer you examine them, the better you'll understand your Original and what has shaped their lives.

(to all)

So, who wants to start us off? Stevenson…how about it?

*(**SANDRA** sits up straight and closes her eyes.)*

COUNSELOR SUE. Concentrate. Dig far. Dig deep. A moment in time.

*(The lights fade, as a spotlight comes up on **SANDRA**.)*

SANDRA. Farmington Lake. It's hot. Almost melting the Jell-O that Mother made. I've just helped set the table and Father and the boys are playing catch. The wind picks up and Mother tells me to put the silverware on the plates and napkins so they won't blow away. She smiles at me and tells me how special I am and how much help I've been to her. I notice, maybe for the first time, how much I look like her. We have the same eyes. It's like looking at a reflection of myself.

(The lights come back up on the whole scene.)

COUNSELOR SUE. Excellent. Very nice.

*(to **WENDY**)*

Merris, your turn. Dig far. Dig deep. A moment in time.

*(Lights down again, this time the spot is on **WENDY**. She closes her eyes and concentrates for a moment.)*

WENDY. Two days before Christmas. I was 6 years old. On my best behavior because I wanted a Jinsa Doll. Mom and Dad were over at the Lowells for a Christmas Party and had left me with Grandma. She fell asleep within a half-hour and that's when I went snooping. My parents were not very good at hiding things, so I found the stash in just minutes. There it was…a Jinsa Doll. I thought I did a pretty good job of acting like I was surprised on Christmas Day when I unwrapped it.

(Lights back up.)

COUNSELOR SUE. Remember that, Merris. Your Original cares about others' feelings. She wanted her parents to think that she was completely surprised and delighted, even though she already knew about the doll.

*(to **MICHAEL**)*

Allen, why don't you give it a try.

MICHAEL. I've never done it before.

COUNSELOR SUE. It's easy. Don't try to think of anything. Just let your mind open up until a memory surfaces above all others. Concentrate. Dig far. Dig deep. A moment in time.

(Lights down, spot on **MICHAEL**. *He closes his eyes and tips his head back a bit. Digging much further than the others.)*

MICHAEL. The smell in Mr. Armstrong's science class was a cross between cheap industrial wax and rancid ammonia. The previous day we had all been given a jar. Wide mouthed. Pint type jars. The kind that have an airtight lid. At the bottom of each jar we were told to put about two inches of dry sawdust. In a separate container we mixed five teaspoons of plaster of Paris with water, just thin enough to pour. The wet plaster was then poured over the sawdust to a depth of about one and one half inches. 24 hours later the plaster had dried and the jars were ready for the final step. Mr. Armstrong didn't tell us why we were making these jars…most of us just thought it was another one of his stupid experiments. He went to each of us and looked at our jars and then poured some ethyl acetate into each one… well he called it that, but the girls all knew it as fingernail polish remover. We thought maybe it would cause a chemical reaction when mixed with the plaster and sawdust, but it didn't. After a few minutes the acetate soaked down into the sawdust and he finally told us what we had just made. A killing jar. Designed to dispatch insects quickly. It was all about death and Mr. Armstrong was loving every minute of it. He crossed to the window and opened it, revealing the most perfect day ever right outside. We could see dozens of butterflies hovering around a Milkweed plant that we later found out he planted just for the purpose of attracting big colorful Monarch butterflies. Mr. Armstrong grabbed a net that he had in the corner of the room and reached it out the window and caught a helpless Monarch. He puffed his chest out in some sort of sick dominant superiority. Clutching the net with his free hand he came straight over to my desk and told me to open the killing jar. Everyone was looking at me and even though I didn't want to, I did it anyway. He placed the butterfly into the jar and quickly fastened down the lid. The other kids came running over to watch as the Monarch frantically tried to escape the prison. It didn't take long until it succumbed to the poison and its beautiful stained glass looking wings stopped moving. It was death. We all got to watch it. And it all happened in a jar that I had made. A killing jar.

(Lights back on stage. They all stare at **MICHAEL**.*)*

ZOOM. Whoa. That was intense.

WENDY. I thought they removed all the really bad memories before the upload.

COUNSELOR SUE. Uh...well...that wasn't really a bad memory...it was more like a science project that had an impact on Allen's Original.

(An electronic buzzer is heard. The Copies get up from their chairs and head for the door.)

COUNSELOR SUE. Allen, I need to talk to you for a moment.

*(***MICHAEL*** stops. The others leave.)*

MICHAEL. I'm sorry, it was the first memory that hit me.

COUNSELOR SUE. This has nothing to do with your memory. Well, maybe it does in a way. Although I wouldn't talk about that one when you get to meet your Original... next Tuesday.

MICHAEL. That's only four days away. This is wonderful news. I was worried because I hadn't heard anything and they promised it would be within the first week.

COUNSELOR SUE. Lately it's been averaging more like two or three weeks before the first meeting.

MICHAEL. The important thing is that I'm going to meet him.

COUNSELOR SUE. That doesn't mean you'll be leaving us.

MICHAEL. He'll want to take me home...I just know it!

Scene Eight

(Cottage #4 – Main Area. A few days later. Offstage voices are heard.)

VOICES. I don't know, but I've been told
Copies never get too old
We may have their DNA
But we're made to throw away.

*(The Copies now enter the scene, lead by **MELISSA**. They break formation and enjoy a good laugh.)*

WENDY. I completely flunked that test today.

SANDRA. That was the toughest one yet.

BETTY. I'm afraid I didn't make the grade.

ZOOM. None of us did…'cept Michael.

WENDY. Yeah, way to throw off the curve, genius.

MICHAEL. I apologize, but I really can't help it.

MELISSA. Don't any of you get it yet? It doesn't matter.

WENDY. What doesn't matter?

MELISSA. The test. It means nothing.

SANDRA. We get graded on it. That means something.

MELISSA. So, who sees those grades?

MICHAEL. Our Originals.

MELISSA. That's a big lie. Used to keep us in line.

MICHAEL. How do you know they don't show them our grades?

MELISSA. There's a lot I know that you Copies don't.

(She holds up a key.)

BETTY. Hickory dickory dock…she's got a key to a lock.

MELISSA. That's right, Betty. While you Copies are sleeping, Melissa has gone creeping.

*(**BETTY** applauds the rhyme.)*

WENDY. What does that open?

MELISSA. Everything. It's a master key.

SANDRA. How did you get it?

MELISSA. My secret.

ZOOM. You got access to everything around here and you didn't tell us?

MELISSA. I'm telling you now.

ZOOM. Let's go do some stuff with it.

MELISSA. What do you have in mind, Zoom?

ZOOM. Uh…oh, I know…we could go into the cafeteria and put sugar in the salt shakers.

(Everyone looks at ZOOM.)

MELISSA. Now you see why I've kept this to myself.

WENDY. How about we go spy on the other cottages?

MELISSA. The only thing I'm going to use this key for is to get out.

WENDY. Get out of where?

MELISSA. Camp I.M.U.

(The others are all stunned at that.)

SANDRA. The only way to leave this place is with your Original. And Melissa you're not exactly building a good bridge with yours.

MELISSA. I can't stand my Original.

MICHAEL. Melissa, don't say that.

MELISSA. Why? It's true. And it's pretty clear that she feels the same way about me.

SANDRA. Your Original wants you. It's just going to take a little longer in your case.

MELISSA. Now you sound like Counselor Sue. And every other leader in this camp that drills that into our heads.

MICHAEL. Your Original's family wouldn't have ordered you if they didn't really want you.

SANDRA. Yes, they need you.

MELISSA. Oh, she needs me alright. But it isn't because of my friendship.

WENDY. She needs you to do things for her.

MELISSA. It's more than that.

WENDY. What are you talking about?

(**MELISSA** *crosses to look out to make sure the coast is clear. She then talks to them in a hushed tone.*)

MELISSA. This key has given me access to something that I suspected all along. The real reason we were created...

(*She has everyone's attention.*)

MELISSA. Spare parts.

SANDRA. You don't know that's true.

MELISSA. I found some records. Copies that left this camp and went right to the Harvesting Centers.

WENDY. They told us that happens sometimes. But only to Unwanteds...or in case of an extreme emergency.

ZOOM. Yeah...like hardly ever.

MELISSA. A lot more than any of us thought.

SANDRA. You're just trying to scare us, Melissa. We're here for orientation and then we're going to live with our Originals.

MELISSA. Yeah, well so what if we do go live with our Originals? How long do you think we have before they need our body parts? 5 years? 10? 20? There are a million and one things that can go wrong with an Original's body. Maybe we'll be lucky and it will only be one kidney. Or just a pint or two of blood to build up their reserve. But what if they need our heart? Or something else that we can't live without?

MICHAEL. We should be glad to help them.

MELISSA. We only feel that way because it was programmed into us. Well, I for one am not going to be somebody's portable parts department. I'm getting out of here.

WENDY. When?

MELISSA. Soon.

ZOOM. You'll never make it.

MELISSA. I think I will.

SANDRA. Where will you go? Do you even have a plan?

MELISSA. Of course I have a plan. I'm going to fight for Copy Rights.

ZOOM. You're gonna copyright your plan?

MELISSA. Not copyright…a Copy's Rights. I'm going straight to the top and protest.

SANDRA. The top of what?

MELISSA. The top of whatever. The media. The government. Whoever will listen to me. I'm planning on blowing the roof right off this compound and exposing it for what it is?

MICHAEL. What exactly are you going to expose?

MELISSA. All of this. The imprisonment. The meetings with our Originals that don't work out. The oppression. The harvesting. All the stuff we have to suffer with.

SANDRA. I'm not suffering.

MELISSA. How do you know? All you have…all that any of us have is someone else's memories. This is just another big lab where they're controlling everything about us.

ZOOM. She's got a good point. What about *our* rights?

MELISSA. Exactly. We deserve our freedom.

WENDY. Why should I have to put on weight? Copy rights now!

BETTY. Hell no, she won't grow!

WENDY. Why should we have to please our Originals? How about making them please us!

MELISSA. What do we want?

WENDY & ZOOM. Freedom!

MELISSA. When do we want it?

WENDY & ZOOM. Now!

BETTY. Wow!

MELISSA. We can make a difference…all of us. I've been practicing my speeches in isolation. They think I was talking to myself, but I was talking to you and you and you and all the Copies who have suffered. It's time we spoke up…it's time we spoke out. Things are gonna change around here!

(**MELISSA** *leads them all in a chant that reaches a fevered pitch.*)

WENDY & ZOOM & MELISSA. Copy rights! Copy rights! Copy rights!

MELISSA. So who's going with me?

(*They all stop chanting and look at* **MELISSA**.)

WENDY. You want us to break out of here with you?

MELISSA. Absolutely.

(*They have all lost the enthusiasm.*)

MELISSA. I don't believe this…

(*to* **ZOOM**)

Come with me, Zoom…we'll score the touchdown of a lifetime.

ZOOM. I would…but it's my turn to pick a movie for movie night.

(*crosses to* **WENDY**)

MELISSA. You won't have to force feed yourself anymore.

WENDY. I'm feeling really bloated right now. I'd just slow you down.

(*crosses to* **BETTY**)

MELISSA. We could try to get you un-redesigned so you'd be back to your old self.

(**BETTY** *looks at the others; speaks for them all.*)

BETTY. We're going to stay here, driven mainly by our fear.

(**MELISSA** *crosses to* **MICHAEL** *and* **SANDRA**.)

MELISSA. Guess I don't have to ask you two.

SANDRA. It's like Betty said. We're afraid, Melissa. We weren't created to fight for ourselves.

MICHAEL. My Original's Dad is a lawyer. After I go home with him tomorrow…

ZOOM. You ain't goin' home with him.

SANDRA. He might.

MICHAEL. Maybe in time I can ask him to take up your cause. He might be able to find a legal reason to change some things.

MELISSA. I can't wait that long.

(We hear a chiming sound.)

WENDY. Nutrition time!

(They are all happy about that and head to towards the exit, avoiding eye contact with **MELISSA** *as they leave.)*

MELISSA. I will leave this place. With or without you.

(They are now gone. **MELISSA** *stands on stage alone as the lights fade out on her.)*

Scene Nine

(Greeting Room "B." The next day. There is a small table with two chairs. **MICHAEL** *is pacing and* **SANDRA** *sits in one of the chairs.)*

SANDRA. Maybe we should go check at the front desk again.

MICHAEL. He'll be here. They're just running behind schedule. Dad is always behind schedule.

SANDRA. Three hours?

MICHAEL. Sometimes. He might have been tied up in court or something. I'm sure they'll tell me all about it on the ride home because…

(He stops when he hears the sound of a door opening.)

MICHAEL. It's him…he's here!

*(***COUNSELOR SUE*** enters.)*

COUNSELOR SUE. I've been looking all over for you two. I thought you were going to wait in my office.

MICHAEL. We decided that being here would give me a better chance to acclimate myself to the room before his arrival.

COUNSELOR SUE. Stevenson, why don't you wait outside.

SANDRA. By myself?

COUNSELOR SUE. You won't be alone…Counselor Adam is at the Reception desk.

SANDRA. Yes Ma'am.

*(***SANDRA*** exits.)*

COUNSELOR SUE. Allen, about your Original…

MICHAEL. Running late is he? That's my Original. Probably the main reason he needs me. Always late for things. Just like Dad. I was just telling Stevenson that they probably got detained in traffic…

COUNSELOR SUE. We called the family a few minutes ago.

MICHAEL. Called them? They aren't home because they're on their way here.

COUNSELOR SUE. They were home.

(**MICHAEL** *is starting to realize.*)

MICHAEL. They're still at home? All of them?

COUNSELOR SUE. They've changed their mind, Allen.

MICHAEL. Today's bad for them? Okay, well…when did they reschedule? I can certainly wait a day or two more.

COUNSELOR SUE. They've decided to cancel the order.

(*Long pause as* **MICHAEL** *processes that.*)

MICHAEL. I don't understand. They've never even met me.

COUNSELOR SUE. This happens sometimes. People order and pay for a clone and then change their minds.

MICHAEL. But you said they had scheduled the first appointment.

COUNSELOR SUE. Sometimes they have a change of heart between when they schedule and the day of the first meeting. I'm as surprised as you are. They don't usually wait until the last minute like this…

MICHAEL. Was it my Original? Is Robert the one that doesn't want me?

COUNSELOR SUE. I didn't talk to the Allens personally. They won't let Counselors do that. I'm just passing on what I was told.

MICHAEL. This is not logical. I can't believe that he wouldn't want me.

COUNSELOR SUE. It probably has nothing to do with him. The parents are the ones that ordered you and in most cases they are the ones who are responsible for canceling the order.

(**MICHAEL** *thinks for a moment.*)

MICHAEL. So, what's going to happen to me?

COUNSELOR SUE. You'll stay here. Nothing will change. There have been many cases where, with a little pressure from us, the families decide to go through with it after all. Our "Persuasion Team" will work very hard to make that happen.

MICHAEL. How long do they keep Unwanteds around here? I mean, if all your extra efforts fail and the Allens don't change their minds…how long before I'm…harvested?

COUNSELOR SUE. You shouldn't even think about that now.

MICHAEL. How long?

COUNSELOR SUE. I can't give you a specific time frame.

MICHAEL. I know you're just trying to make me feel better but you don't have to. I was created to process the truth. I know that when a clone outlasts their usefulness, or is an "Unwanted," they get harvested. I can deal with that.

COUNSELOR SUE. Even if they never come here to claim you, it doesn't mean you will be harvested. The best thing you can do is to keep up with your studies and let our team of professionals do their job. They're really good at what they do.

(**MICHAEL** *does not respond.*)

COUNSELOR SUE. Come on, I'll walk you back to your cottage.

MICHAEL. No thank you. I wish to be alone now.

COUNSELOR SUE. Allen, being alone…that's not a good idea. You know that.

MICHAEL. Right now it's a very good idea. And please don't call me Allen…

(*pointed*)

…my name is Michael.

(**COUNSELOR SUE** *exits. Lights slowly fade.*)

Scene Ten

(Cottage #4 – Main Area. One hour later. **SANDRA**, **WENDY**, **ZOOM** *and* **BETTY** *watch as* **MELISSA** *points to a large unfolded map.)*

MELISSA. I wait here for the night and then travel along this road and cut over here to the city.

ZOOM. Why not just hit this main road and hitchhike into the city?

WENDY. Zoom, use the few brain cells the lab gave you why don't you? Someone might pick her up and report her to the police or something.

SANDRA. Maybe the next meeting with your Original will go better.

MELISSA. By the time my next meeting rolls around, I'll be long gone.

*(***WENDY*** hands* **MELISSA** *some cash.)*

WENDY. Not much here but it might be enough to pay for a night or two at a Motel.

MELISSA. Where did you get this?

WENDY. My Original's mom gave it to me. Extra food money.

MELISSA. Thanks.

*(***ZOOM*** hands her a Swiss Army knife.)*

ZOOM. Here. You may need this.

MELISSA. I can't take this, Zoom. Your Original gave it to you.

ZOOM. Well...not really...I kinda took it.

SANDRA. You stole from your Original?

ZOOM. It's what he woulda done.

*(***BETTY*** thinks of something and pulls a nutrition bar from her pocket.)*

BETTY. You can go far with this "vitamin packed" Energy Bar.

MELISSA. Thanks, Betty.

SANDRA. I don't have anything to give you, Melissa…except my good thoughts that your journey is safe.

MELISSA. That just might be the thing I need the most.

(to others)

I need all of you to do that.

WENDY. And lie, too. When the Counselors find out Melissa broke out of here the first place they're going to come asking questions is right here.

SANDRA. I don't think I can lie.

ZOOM. It's easy…

MELISSA. None of you will have to lie. Tell them the truth. By the time I'm gone then it won't matter.

ZOOM. Uh…but you showed us the map of where you were goin'.

*(**MELISSA** starts to fold up the map with a mischievous grin.)*

MELISSA. That's right. It's the route I want you to tell them about.

*(**SANDRA** and **WENDY** realize what she means by that.)*

ZOOM. *(confused)* If we tell them, then they'll follow you.

SANDRA. Melissa just told us that so if they asked us we wouldn't have to lie and it would throw them off the trail.

ZOOM. Oh, yeah…I knew that.

SANDRA. When are you leaving?

MELISSA. Better not tell you that either. Let's just say that it will be very soon.

BETTY. Before Melissa becomes the dearly departed, I say we get this party started.

MELISSA. Party?

WENDY. Yeah, we thought we'd give you a going away party.

ZOOM. Party!

WENDY. One thing we do have around here…is plenty of party snacks.

(WENDY crosses to her big bag of junk food. Starts passing out candy and chips to everyone.)

ZOOM. A party ain't a party without music? Betty…bongos!

BETTY. I got the beat so you can shuffle your feet.

(BETTY crosses over to a cube and begins to pound on it like a bongo drum. The others start to dance. SANDRA stops cold when she sees something and it takes the others a moment or two before they realize why she has stopped. BETTY is the last to see MICHAEL enter and stops banging on the cube.)

SANDRA. Michael, what happened? Did they finally show up? Are you going home?

WENDY. Does it look like he's going home?

SANDRA. Maybe he's just here to pick up his things. Is that it Michael?

MICHAEL. No. I'm not going home…

ZOOM. Ha-ha…He didn't make it. Just like we told him.

SANDRA. That's enough, Zoom.

(ZOOM crosses to MICHAEL.)

ZOOM. Mr. High IQ here thought he was so much better'n the rest of us. Thought he'd get to go home on the first meeting.

(in MICHAEL's face)

How you like the smell of reality, Copy?

MELISSA. Mute it, Zoom.

ZOOM. You're takin' his side? After all his big talk?

MELISSA. Not taking anyone's side. Just telling you to shut up.

(MICHAEL sits on a cube. SANDRA crosses to him.)

SANDRA. Don't let it get you down. You'll go home with him next time.

BETTY. You know what to do…just wait for meeting #2.

WENDY. Yeah, next time you'll do it.

(**MICHAEL** *stands up and crosses to* **MELISSA**.)

MICHAEL. May I speak with you, Melissa?

MELISSA. Go ahead.

MICHAEL. I mean just you and me…privately.

MELISSA. Yeah, okay.

(to others)

All right you malformed misfits…vacate.

ZOOM. Come on…we want to hear the whole story.

MELISSA. I said vacate…Now!

(*They all know better than to challenge* **MELISSA**. **ZOOM**, **WENDY**, **SANDRA**, *and* **BETTY** *exit*.)

MELISSA. Didn't go very well, did it?

MICHAEL. That's an understatement.

MELISSA. Never does. They make us think that this orientation thing is just a week or so until our Original comes for us and takes us home.

MICHAEL. And it's my fault for believing that. I was convinced I would be exactly what they wanted.

MELISSA. We all are naïve enough to think that. Then we meet them and they've always got some sort of problem with us. I think it's just a big shock for them. Seeing us. Seeing themselves. Scares 'em a little. Don't know why, I mean they look in the mirror all the time. Same deal. But we always seem to freak them out at the first meeting. So they go home and think about it. Don't worry, they eventually get used to it and take you home.

MICHAEL. I don't think I'm going to get that far.

MELISSA. You will. I didn't figure you'd get it the first meeting, but a Copy like you…with what you have to offer…I bet the next meeting will be the deal.

MICHAEL. There won't be a next meeting…because there wasn't a first meeting.

MELISSA. They didn't make it?

MICHAEL. No.

MELISSA. That's not good. So when did they reschedule?

MICHAEL. They're not going to.

(**MELISSA** *looks at him for a moment and then realizes.*)

MELISSA. They cancelled the order?

MICHAEL. Yes. Counselor Sue told me it was pretty rare since they don't get their money back if they cancel.

MELISSA. Not only that…if they ever need you for parts they've given up all rights to that.

MICHAEL. I know, even if they don't want me you'd think they'd keep me around in case some day they need me.

MELISSA. Maybe they'll change their mind…you know… later.

MICHAEL. Unlikely.

MELISSA. Sorry to hear about it.

MICHAEL. Look, I don't want your sympathy. That's not why I wanted to talk to you.

MELISSA. And you won't get any sympathy from me either. All of us here got problems with our Originals.

MICHAEL. Yes, I know. However, I'm the only Unwanted here.

MELISSA. Come on, you know what they say here at Camp I.M.U.: "Don't think of yourself as unwanted…think of yourself as special."

MICHAEL. You sound just like a Counselor.

MELISSA. You don't know how many times I've heard that speech. "You clones are special, because your Originals *wanted* you to be made." You know they hacked that from some old adoption agency book. They used to tell adopted kids that their new parents loved them more because they "chose" them. Maybe it worked for the poor orphans but it's nothing but a sound byte for us Copies. We're not special. We're spare parts with an attitude. They don't love us. They ordered us. Like so much furniture.

MICHAEL. All of you were right, I never should have been so positive about the success of my first meeting.

MELISSA. Don't worry about Zoom going all mitosis on you about this…I'll make sure he doesn't.

MICHAEL. I'm not worried about that…because I don't plan on sticking around here.

MELISSA. What are you talking about?

MICHAEL. I want to escape with you.

MELISSA. Whoa, I don't think so.

MICHAEL. Yesterday you asked us if we wanted to come.

MELISSA. I was mainly asking Wendy and Zoom.

MICHAEL. Take me with you. I can be of invaluable assistance.

MELISSA. How?

MICHAEL. I'm pretty good in the outdoors. My Original did a lot of hiking in the wilderness.

MELISSA. I'm good in the outdoors, too.

MICHAEL. You wouldn't have to be alone.

MELISSA. That's not a problem for me. Why do you think I spent so much time in isolation?

MICHAEL. You messed up a lot.

MELISSA. I messed up on purpose. Each time they put me in there it made me stronger. It's like practicing to hold your breath underwater…you build up time.

MICHAEL. You won't have to hold your breath…I'll be there with you.

MELISSA. Traveling with someone might slow me down. I'd spend most of my time having to deal with your issues.

MICHAEL. The only "issue" I had decided to cancel me today. I'm an Unwanted…I have nothing to lose.

(MELISSA looks at him for a moment.)

MELISSA. Maybe that's what worries me the most.

MICHAEL. I promise I won't hold you back.

MELISSA. Well…

MICHAEL. There's only one thing I ask.

MELISSA. Here we go.

MICHAEL. We make one side trip...to see my Original and his family.

MELISSA. You want to see them after what they did to you?

MICHAEL. I have to find out why they didn't want me. I don't want to be harvested without knowing what made them cancel me.

MELISSA. You know, as weird as that sounds...I can understand your point.

MICHAEL. So you'll take me with you?

(**MELISSA** *thinks long and hard. She looks around to make sure no one is listening.*)

MELISSA. *(whispers)* I plan on leaving...tonight...at Midnight. If you're not ready...I'll go without you.

MICHAEL. I'll be ready.

MELISSA. We both better get a few hours of recharging.

(She starts to head off.)

MICHAEL. Melissa...Thank you...I don't feel so Unwanted anymore.

(They both exit.)

Scene Eleven

(Cottage #4 – Bunk Area #2. 0200 hours. **ZOOM** *and* **WENDY** *are both asleep.* **BETTY** *sits on the floor reading. She is surprised to see* **SANDRA** *enter.)*

SANDRA. Betty, would you come stay with me in my room?
BETTY. Now? Holy cow.

*(***WENDY*** wakes up and sees ***SANDRA***.)*

WENDY. What's the event?
SANDRA. Michael's gone.
WENDY. Gone? Where?

*(***ZOOM*** is awake now.)*

SANDRA. With Melissa.
ZOOM. Melissa left already?
BETTY. Why do you think I'm here, my dear?
ZOOM. No way Michael went with Melissa.
WENDY. Did you see him leave?
SANDRA. No. I woke up and he was gone. He left me this note.

*(***SANDRA*** holds up a hand written note. ***WENDY*** grabs it from her and reads it.)*

SANDRA. "Sandra, I've decided to leave with Melissa and I think you will understand why. Michael."

*(***WENDY*** takes the letter and looks at it.)*

ZOOM. I still don't believe it.
WENDY. 'specially since he never liked to use the name Michael.
SANDRA. He changed his mind about that after yesterday.
ZOOM. So what happened at his meeting? Bet even his Original thought he was a Dolly.
SANDRA. They cancelled him….
WENDY. I thought his first meeting just went bad. Like they always do.

SANDRA. It went bad all right. So bad he had to leave here.

BETTY. His meeting had no greeting.

SANDRA. I guess I might consider the same thing if I found out I was cancelled.

ZOOM. Yeah, me too.

WENDY. One thing's for sure. Now that Michael's an Unwanted if they catch him…he'll be harvested immediately.

Scene Twelve

(At the same time. Somewhere out on the road. **MICHAEL** *and* **MELISSA** *stop for a moment to catch their breath.)*

MICHAEL. I can't believe we just walked out of there like that.

MELISSA. Yeah, easier than I thought it would be.

MICHAEL. Well, the key helped.

MELISSA. Only had to use it on one door. Even without the key we could have gotten out.

MICHAEL. They really need to consider upgrading their security.

MELISSA. Why? Think about it. You got a whole compound full of Copies whose only goal in life is to go home with their Originals. They don't want to break out. No one's ever wanted to.

MICHAEL. Until we did. We'll be legends.

MELISSA. I don't think anyone will understand why we did this. Not really sure I understand.

MICHAEL. You did it to fight for Copy Rights.

MELISSA. It's just that I'm not sure what my one voice will be able to do.

MICHAEL. There will be two voices. I'll be right there with you…that is after I find out why my Original cancelled me.

MELISSA. Think they'll tell you the real reason?

MICHAEL. I don't know. But I have to try.

MELISSA. Guess that's my reason, too.

(beat)

Now we better keep moving.

*(***MICHAEL*** looks around.)*

MICHAEL. Wait a minute…

MELISSA. What?

MICHAEL. It appears that we've come full circle.

(MELISSA looks around.)

MICHAEL. Recognize that tree? Remember, you said it looked like a giant Praying Mantis.

MELISSA. You're right.

(MICHAEL unfolds the map and looks at it.)

MICHAEL. I see what happened. We should have gone toward that mountain peak over there.

(He points. MELISSA looks at the map.)

MELISSA. Damn it to Dolly. We must have lost at least two hours.

MICHAEL. It's okay, Melissa…time is one thing we have a lot of.

(They exit.)

Scene Thirteen

(Cottage #4 – Bunk Area #2. 0300 hours. **ZOOM** *and* **WENDY** *are both pretending to be asleep.)*

ZOOM. Wendy, you asleep?

WENDY. Yes.

ZOOM. Oh, okay…sorry.

*(***WENDY** *shakes her head in disbelief.)*

WENDY. Obviously if I was asleep I'd not be able to answer you.

(beat)

You worried about Melissa and Michael, too?

ZOOM. Yeah, what if they get caught?

WENDY. Might be the best thing for them.

ZOOM. What?

WENDY. I mean, compared to what they face trying to fight the Originals.

ZOOM. If anybody can do it, Melissa can.

WENDY. This might even be too much for her. I don't think the Originals want to hear from a Copy.

ZOOM. Melissa's gonna change all that.

WENDY. I don't know. Maybe we should have gone with her. She can't do it all alone.

ZOOM. She's got Michael.

WENDY. I just don't know if that's going to be enough.

ZOOM. We could go right now?

WENDY. What?

ZOOM. You and me. We could break outta here, too.

WENDY. Yeah, we could catch up to them and then the four of us could work together to change things.

ZOOM. Yeah!

WENDY. So let's do it.

(Long pause as they both think about it.)

WENDY. Well, I am kind of tired tonight…and it is really late.

ZOOM. Oh…uh…yeah, I'm tired too.

WENDY. We'll do it tomorrow, or something.

ZOOM. Yeah, tomorrow…

(They look at each other for a long moment and then roll over and go back to pretending they are asleep.)

Scene Fourteen

(Somewhere else out on the road. 0400 hours. **MELISSA** *enters supporting* **MICHAEL** *who limps badly. Exhausted they stop for a moment and* **MICHAEL** *sits.)*

MICHAEL. I can't believe a little hole in the ground could do this kind of damage.

MELISSA. Let me see it.

*(***MICHAEL** *takes off his shoe.* **MELISSA** *examines his ankle.)*

MELISSA. It's swelling by the second.

MICHAEL. It's not broken.

MELISSA. Might as well be.

*(***MICHAEL** *stands, trying to hide the pain, then quickly sits back down.)*

MICHAEL. Just give me a few minutes, I'll be better. I promise.

*(***MELISSA** *looks off at the horizon.)*

MELISSA. See that glow way off there?

MICHAEL. It's beautiful…like a giant night-light.

MELISSA. That's the city where we're going.

MICHAEL. It's like they lit it up just for us.

MELISSA. A city full of Originals. Living their lives. Day after day. And taking it all for granted.

MICHAEL. Do you ever wonder what it would be like to have been born instead of made?

MELISSA. All the time.

MICHAEL. Counselor Sue says we're luckier than Originals because they get all hung up on why they're here…at least we know why we were created.

*(***MELISSA** *looks at* **MICHAEL** *for a moment.)*

MELISSA. Remember when you were being initiated.

MICHAEL. Of course, that would be something hard to forget.

MELISSA. When we did that kissing thing...you know...

MICHAEL. "Search the urge."

MELISSA. Right...well, when you kissed me...I kinda felt something.

MICHAEL. You did?

MELISSA. Well, I don't think it was love...not how the Originals describe it anyway...but I did feel something.

MICHAEL. Did it feel like for the first time you cared for someone? Not based on a memory that was uploaded in you, but it was something you yourself felt...all on your own?

MELISSA. *(surprised)* Yes, that's exactly how I felt.

MICHAEL. I know...I felt that way, too.

MELISSA. Why didn't you say something?

MICHAEL. Because I didn't understand what I was feeling. Why didn't you?

MELISSA. Same reason...and it kinda scared me.

(beat)

Uh...we should keep moving. Do you think you can make it?

MICHAEL. Yes.

*(**MICHAEL** stands up, takes two steps and falls down. He writhes on the ground holding his ankle.)*

MELISSA. You can't even walk on it.

MICHAEL. You must proceed without me.

MELISSA. I can't do that, Michael.

MICHAEL. You have to. I'm just going to hold you up. We'll be caught for sure.

MELISSA. And what will you do?

MICHAEL. Go back to Camp I.M.U.

MELISSA. How are you going to do that? Crawl? On that bad bone it'll take you days.

*(**MELISSA** crosses over to **MICHAEL** and helps him to his feet. She put his arm around her neck.)*

MICHAEL. It's no use I can't go on. It's too far...

MELISSA. We're not going on...we're going back to the Camp.

MICHAEL. But you've been planning this for so long. I can't let you lose all that.

MELISSA. I'm just going to drop you off. Then I'll take off again on my own. I'm not losing anything except a little time. And like you said, we got plenty of that.

(The two head off.)

Scene Fifteen

(Cottage #4 – Main Area. 2 weeks later. **ZOOM**, **WENDY**, **SANDRA** *and* **BETTY** *are hovered around a now familiar floor area on the stage. This time they are not tapping, but listening to someone tapping to them.* **WENDY** *counts while* **SANDRA** *writes down the letters on a piece of paper.)*

WENDY. 19…

SANDRA. S…

WENDY. 15…

SANDRA. O…

WENDY. 15 again…

SANDRA. O…

WENDY. 14…

SANDRA. N…

*(***WENDY*** listens. Nothing more.)*

WENDY. That's it. What did he say?

SANDRA. "Soon."

WENDY. What does he mean by that? What about soon?

ZOOM. He's escaping!

SANDRA. Again?

WENDY. Not from isolation. Not possible.

BETTY. Soon he'll be here…and that's cause for cheer!

SANDRA. Very good, Betty. Michael's getting out of isolation and will "soon" be here.

WENDY. We'll have a party.

ZOOM. Yeah. Party!

WENDY. Except we don't have any snacks.

ZOOM. Don't you got any leftovers?

WENDY. No, I tossed them all after I found out Carla went on that new Australian diet.

SANDRA. Well, I bet it will be easier for you to lose weight than to gain it.

WENDY. Eight pounds already.

(She poses.)

BETTY. Lose weight now…ask her how.

ZOOM. *(sarcasm)* Yeah, she's practically a bone.

SANDRA. Well I noticed it, Wendy. And I bet Michael will, too.

WENDY. Can't believe he's in isolation…again. That's the second time this week.

BETTY. He's been acting whack, since he came back.

WENDY. Can you blame him? He's an Unwanted. That would take the frosting off anybody's cake.

SANDRA. Maybe they redesigned him. He behaves so badly most of the time.

WENDY. Like they'd redesign him to be bad?

SANDRA. It would give them a reason to harvest him sooner.

WENDY. I don't think they need a reason. If they want to strip him of his parts they can do it anytime they want. Besides, I like the new Michael. Now that Melissa is gone we need someone around here to remind us not to be such Dollys all the time.

BETTY. Dolly…Dolly…Golly Dolly Folly Molly Holly Jolly Polly Volley Wally Golly Dolly Molly Holly Jolly…

*(They all look at **BETTY** who continues the "olly" outburst.)*

WENDY. I think she's stuck or something.

*(**BETTY** smacks herself in the head and stops her outburst.)*

BETTY. Oops, I looped.

(She's fine now.)

WENDY. Now that Michael's ankle has healed he'll break out of here again and go find Melissa.

SANDRA. Won't be easy to do that again. Ever since they found out Melissa left here they've added more security.

ZOOM. Melissa gave him the key.
SANDRA. Useless, they changed all the locks.
WENDY. I bet Michael will find another way out.
ZOOM. Yeah, Michael's the number one.

Scene Sixteen

(Isolation area. **MICHAEL** *sits in the red chair in deep thought. After several long moments he removes his recording device from his pocket, speaks into it.)*

MICHAEL. Robert, this will be my last audio journal entry mainly because I don't think you'll ever hear anything I've recorded anyway. But in case you do, I wanted to tell you something I have learned about myself. *(pause)* When I was first created I was an exact copy of you. In every way. I looked like you, talked like you, and with the memories they uploaded I even thought like you. From my point of awareness my only purpose for being was to serve you and I wanted nothing more than to do that. *(pause)* But I don't feel that way anymore. Being here at this camp has given me my own experiences, my own friends, and my own thoughts. I have also been lucky enough to meet someone who showed me that I can be an individual and not just a Copy. You Originals always talk about freedom and choice and how important independence is. I'm starting to see that none of you really understand what those words mean. *(pause)* I now realize that even though I was created from you, I have become every bit my own person. Whatever little time I have left will be my time. To fill with my experiences and think my thoughts. I am Michael. And that's something no one can take away.

*(***MICHAEL*** clicks the device off.)*

Scene Seventeen

(Back in Cottage #4. One hour later.)

ZOOM. Gotta give ten-ups to Michael for not sayin' anything about Melissa.

WENDY. Yeah, I thought for sure he'd tell them everything about where she went.

SANDRA. Michael would never do that. He's stronger than all of us.

WENDY. You're right about that…two weeks and he hasn't broken yet.

ZOOM. And neither have we.

WENDY. Melissa would be proud of all of us.

SANDRA. We need to be careful. If our Originals find out we lied…

WENDY. We didn't lie…we just told them we didn't know anything.

BETTY. The rule of thumb is just to act dumb.

SANDRA. We knew about them leaving.

WENDY. But not where they went. Only Michael knew the details. And his Original could care less if he lied about that.

ZOOM. Hey, let's tell Michael about that email from Melissa.

(He grabs the broom and is about to tap on the floor. **WENDY** *stops him.)*

WENDY. No, too dangerous.

SANDRA. Too close to nutrition time for him.

BETTY. Yeah, Zoom, put down that broom.

*(***ZOOM*** decides to set the broom aside.)*

WENDY. Besides, we don't really know if that email was from her.

ZOOM. 'Course it was.

SANDRA. It was a spam ad for Valium.

ZOOM. I told you…it's secret code. Valium is medication and that starts with the letter "M" just like Melissa's name…

SANDRA. Come on…

ZOOM. And there were *two* of the very same spam emails. One was a "Copy" of the other one. Get it!

WENDY. I'd like to believe Melissa sent us a message probably even more than you did…but that's really stretching it.

SANDRA. Yeah, and what about that new girl in Cottage #8?

ZOOM. Don't even start with that again. You're just a bunch of doubtin' Dollys.

WENDY. Well, if Melissa is still out there…I don't doubt that she's fighting for our rights. Right now she's probably organizing a big rally or something.

ZOOM. Yeah, she's a born leader.

*(**MICHAEL** enters.)*

MICHAEL. Except she wasn't born. None of us were.

SANDRA. Michael!

*(**MICHAEL** crosses to them and enjoys the same hugs and high-fives **MELISSA** did in an earlier scene when she returned.)*

MICHAEL. Wendy, you look thinner.

WENDY. You see, Zoom…someone noticed!

BETTY. Thinner's a winner.

WENDY. You were in there a long time.

SANDRA. Too long…it's not fair.

WENDY. I don't see how you can handle it. The most I've ever been in isolation was two hours and I just about went daft and a half.

MICHAEL. It's all a matter of concentration. Melissa taught me that. You just need to focus on something and let your mind become your friend. If you use your own thoughts to keep you company then you're never alone.

(The others are impressed with that.)

ZOOM. We heard from Melissa.

MICHAEL. You did?

WENDY. Zoom, don't even start that.

(ZOOM gets close to MICHAEL.)

ZOOM. We got two emails from her – one was a Copy! She disguised them as spam, but I know they were from Melissa.

BETTY. Female email.

MICHAEL. What kind of spam?

ZOOM. Medication…starts with M…just like…

MICHAEL. Melissa.

ZOOM. You get it.

MICHAEL. Could be.

WENDY. You really think so, Michael?

MICHAEL. Anything is possible. Melissa just might do something real subtle like that.

(They all think about that for a moment.)

SANDRA. You know there's also a possibility that Melissa was caught. I heard something…

(MICHAEL crosses to her.)

MICHAEL. What?

SANDRA. A new girl in Cottage #8…

MICHAEL. What about her? Tell me.

SANDRA. Well, some say it's Melissa…redesigned. She arrived here two days after you came back.

MICHAEL. Impossible.

WENDY. Well, I heard that, too…

(quickly)

But I don't believe it for a minute.

SANDRA. I saw her during special assembly. She looked a lot like Melissa…

MICHAEL. Did you talk to her?

SANDRA. No.

MICHAEL. The probability of it being Melissa is incredibly low.

WENDY. Well, the word's out that it's her…and a lot of the Copies here believe it.

(**MICHAEL** *paces for a moment. Looking up at the ceiling.*)

MICHAEL. Oh, they're good all right. I must commend them on their dirty little control tactics. Nice job, people!

SANDRA. Michael, keep your voice down. They might be monitoring.

MICHAEL. The propaganda machine at Camp I.M.U. is working overtime. Don't you see it? They made sure the rumor started that the only Copy to ever escape this camp was caught and redesigned. That new Copy in Cottage #8 is not Melissa. But everyone thinks it is because *they* said so.

(*yelling up to the ceiling*)

You can't fool us. We don't buy it. Melissa is alive and free!

WENDY. Ssshh…Be careful, Michael.

MICHAEL. Why?

SANDRA. You're on probation. They might…

MICHAEL. Harvest me?

SANDRA. Don't even say that word.

MICHAEL. I'm not afraid of it.

SANDRA. Well don't give them a reason to rush it.

ZOOM. Yeah, they might be listening.

BETTY. Their ear might be right here.

MICHAEL. So what? So I get a couple more days sitting and wondering when the big beaker will drop? Losing sleep a couple more nights because I know that my copied DNA will soon be DOA?

(**MICHAEL** *stands up defiantly.*)

MICHAEL. *(shouting)* Bring it on! Let's get it over with. Let's do the "chromosome shuffle." I'm here! What are you waiting for?

SANDRA. Michael, stop. Please.

*(**MICHAEL** stands on the cube and continues to yell at the ceiling. The others ad lib for him to stop.)*

MICHAEL. I'm right here! I'm right here!

*(**MICHAEL** continues and only stops when he notices the others are looking at **COUNSELOR SUE** who has just entered.)*

COUNSELOR SUE. What's going on?

WENDY. Nothing. We were just…

SANDRA. Playing a game.

COUNSELOR SUE. Pretty loud game.

ZOOM. Yeah…it's called… "Loud Game"…uh…you know… who can be the loudest.

*(**COUNSELOR SUE** scrutinizes all of them for a moment. She then walks to **MICHAEL** who is still standing on the cube.)*

COUNSELOR. Allen, come with me.

*(**MICHAEL** hops off the cube.)*

WENDY. He didn't do anything. We were just playing.

MICHAEL. *(to others)* It's okay.

*(He exits with **COUNSELOR SUE**.)*

BETTY. Oh no…say it isn't so.

SANDRA. Maybe she's just taking him to isolation.

ZOOM. More like the "final" isolation.

SANDRA. But he didn't take his belongings. So he's gonna come back. Right?

WENDY. I don't think he'll need his belongings where he's going.

Scene Eighteen

(A meeting room with a small table and two chairs. 10 minutes later. **MICHAEL** *is there with* **COUNSELOR SUE.***)*

MICHAEL. Can I say goodbye to my friends?

COUNSELOR SUE. No. That's against Camp Policy.

MICHAEL. Can I at least have some time to myself before they come for me?

COUNSELOR SUE. If you like, but first there is someone I'm sending in here that you should speak to. It might give you some comfort for what you are going to face.

MICHAEL. Last rights? Well, at least you let us have that. Go ahead, send in the Priest, I've got a few questions I'd like to ask…but I don't think he's going to be able to answer them.

*(***COUNSELOR SUE*** exits.* **MICHAEL** *sits for a moment and then looks up to see* **AMY**, *a 17-year-old Original, who has just entered the room. She gasps when she sees* **MICHAEL.***)*

AMY. Oh my God!

MICHAEL. Amy? What are you doing here?

*(***MICHAEL*** stands up.)*

AMY. I'm…uh…this is incredible. I'm sorry but I didn't think it would be…that you would be…

MICHAEL. So exact?

AMY. Uh…yes…it's amazing. Your face…your voice…

MICHAEL. That happens a lot when Originals see us for the first time. I remember how you reacted to the Schofields when they got their Copy last Christmas.

AMY. Copy?

MICHAEL. Clone.

AMY. Oh. Yeah, I know the Schofields got one…but…

MICHAEL. You're exactly as I remember you, Amy. Or at least as they uploaded me to remember you.

AMY. I am?

MICHAEL. Well you are Robert's sister. They wouldn't leave something like that out. I would need to know you.

AMY. Well, yeah.

MICHAEL. Did Mom and Dad come with you?

AMY. No, I came alone.

MICHAEL. Oh.

(She crosses to **MICHAEL** *and hugs him for a long moment.* **MICHAEL** *is very confused by this.)*

AMY. What should I call you?

MICHAEL. The people here call me Michael.

AMY. Michael?

MICHAEL. *(can't hold back)* Are you here to take me home?

*(***AMY** *doesn't say anything.)*

MICHAEL. I'm sorry. I shouldn't have asked that.

AMY. No, that's okay...I'm here because...because I wanted to apologize...for my parents. It's not like them to do something like this. To just leave you here...but they haven't been themselves lately. At all.

*(***AMY** *stares at him for a moment, still adjusting.)*

MICHAEL. Are you okay, Amy?

AMY. Wow...this is like so hard.

(pause)

On the way over here I had it all planned out how I was going to tell you. I mean, after your Counselor called and told us how hurt you were about how they backed out of the deal and all.

MICHAEL. She called you?

AMY. Yeah.

MICHAEL. She didn't tell me that.

AMY. Well, I explained everything to her. She said she understood but thought we really should contact you. That you'd be wondering. We hadn't even considered that...

MICHAEL. ...that Clones have feelings?

AMY. Right.

MICHAEL. Most Originals don't consider that.

AMY. After I told her about what happened to Robert I think she realized why they cancelled the order.

MICHAEL. What about Robert? What happened?

AMY. She didn't tell you?

MICHAEL. No...What happened to Robert?

(*AMY hadn't counted on this. She sits down in the other chair and collects her thoughts.*)

AMY. I thought you knew...

MICHAEL. No one told me anything. What should I know?

(*long pause*)

MELISSA. There was an accident. At the lake. Robert was too far out. We all thought he was a pretty good swimmer. The lifeguard did what he could...

MICHAEL. What are you saying?

AMY. Robert's dead. He drowned.

(**MICHAEL** *tries to process the information he just heard.*)

AMY. Mom and Dad were completely destroyed. Me, too. I mean all those years Robert and I argued...I'd give anything to go back and just tell him how much I loved the guy.

MICHAEL. (*to himself*) They should have told me...

AMY. When the people at the Camp here called to ask why we hadn't shown up for the meeting with you...Mom and Dad just couldn't deal with it. It was the day of the funeral. We forgot all about the meeting. Actually it kind of scared them that you even existed...you know, someone who looked just like Robert. They just wanted to forget about that. To forget about you. So they cancelled the order.

(*beat*)

Then the other day when your Counselor Melissa called...

(thinking out loud)

AMY. *(cont.)* ...I can't believe she never told you what happened. She seemed really sincere about getting an explanation when she called us.

MICHAEL. Did you say Melissa?

AMY. Yes, Counselor Melissa. She really made a case for you. How wonderful you are. That really impressed me that she'd build you up like that and that she knew you so well. I talked to her the longest because that call really rattled the folks.

(**MICHAEL** *realizes and then smiles.*)

MICHAEL. Yes, Counselor Melissa and I are very close. When exactly did she call you?

AMY. Uh...it was...two days ago.

MICHAEL. So that's not her in Cottage #8.

AMY. What?

MICHAEL. Nothing.

(beat)

I'm really shocked to hear about Robert.

AMY. We were all pretty shocked. I loved him so much.

MICHAEL. I know he never showed it very often but he really cared about you, too.

AMY. He did?

MICHAEL. Remember that time you thought you lost your class ring and then he found it a month later?

AMY. Uh...yes...you know about that? I guess you would.

MICHAEL. It wasn't the actual ring he found. He bought a new one. You were so upset about it so he used his savings and bought it without anyone knowing. It was worth every penny just seeing the look on your face when he handed it to you.

AMY. I never knew that.

MICHAEL. Maybe I shouldn't have told you.

AMY. No, I'm so glad you did.

(**AMY** *looks at* **MICHAEL** *for a moment.*)

AMY. I just can't get over how much you're like him. How real you are. This is gonna take some time.

MICHAEL. Getting used to me?

AMY. Well, that too. But I mean convincing my parents...I mean...our parents...about you.

MICHAEL. Convincing them?

AMY. That we need you...with us.

MICHAEL. You want me to live with you?

AMY. Yes. Not just want...need. I just know if I can get Mom and Dad to come here and talk with you. Well, I don't see how they could not feel the same way I do.

MICHAEL. I was created from Robert to help him, not to replace him.

AMY. I'm not asking you to do that...and neither will they. But you are part of Robert and that makes you part of our family. You belong with us. I know I can convince them of that...just give me a little time.

(**MICHAEL** *takes a moment to process all of this.*)

MICHAEL. Okay, Amy...I'll wait until they're ready. No matter how long it might take for that to happen.

AMY. Really? You're willing to wait?

MICHAEL. Absolutely. But you're going to have to tell the people here that you are rescinding the cancel order. That will make them keep me around here...until you're ready to take me home.

AMY. Yes, of course. Should I talk to Counselor Melissa? I'd really like to meet her.

MICHAEL. She kind of went outside of the rules to talk to you. Do me a favor...just tell the front office...but don't mention her, okay?

AMY. Just like Robert. Always worrying about protecting others. Okay, I won't mention her name.

MICHAEL. Thank you.

AMY. This is a miracle. It's like Robert knew that he wouldn't be around...so he asked for you.

(**AMY** *gives him another hug. This time* **MICHAEL** *hugs back.*)

MICHAEL. Hey, how's Botchy?

AMY. Crazy as ever.

MICHAEL. Still digging up the Nickerson's garden?

AMY. His favorite place to hide his bones. Guess what he did the other day? You know how he likes to grab the mail when the Mailman puts it through the slot…

MICHAEL. That really irritates dad.

AMY. Well, someone mailed dad a really big check and Botchy literally tore it to pieces.

MICHAEL. Uh-oh…talk about being in the dog house!

(Lights fade on the two of them laughing.)

Scene Nineteen

(Cottage #4 – Main Area. Later. **WENDY** *and* **ZOOM** *are huddled around the spot on the floor.* **SANDRA** *holds the broom and is tapping on the floor.* **BETTY** *stands watch.)*

SANDRA. He's not responding.

ZOOM. Maybe he can't. Maybe they beat him up so bad he can't move.

WENDY. Maybe he's not even in there.

SANDRA. He has to be. Where else would they take him?

WENDY. Like I said before…to be harvested.

BETTY. Don't even start saying they stripped him for parts.

ZOOM. Try again, Sandra.

WENDY. I'm telling you he's not there. He would have tapped back by now.

SANDRA. Okay, so he's not there. But that just means he's somewhere else.

ZOOM. Maybe he's helpin' Counselor Sue with somethin'.

WENDY. Get a grasp…Michael's not even in the Camp anymore. By now he's halfway to the Harvesting Center.

SANDRA. I guess that's a possibility, but I just don't want to think that.

WENDY. Do you know what they do to a Copy when they harvest it? From what I hear they don't even put you out all the way. You're conscious as they start pulling out all your useable parts.

SANDRA. That's ridiculous. They're not that cruel.

WENDY. Sure they are…'specially because they look at us as product. No one cares what the product thinks…or feels. They just keep hacking away until they got all the organs they need. They even use the hair cells so some fat bald guy somewhere can have something to comb in the morning. About the only thing they haven't figured out to use is the brain…but they're working on that. And when that happens, look out…we're all headed to the slaughterhouse…

SANDRA. Stop it, Wendy.

ZOOM. Ah, she doesn't know how they harvest Copies. None of us do.

WENDY. I've heard enough stories to know it's true.

BETTY. Only true according to you.

SANDRA. Well, I'm not going to believe any of it…and I'm not going to give up on believing that Michael is still around here.

BETTY. Stop the flapping of your gums, something wicked this way comes.

(They break up and **SANDRA** *ditches the broom.* **COUNSELOR SUE** *enters, followed by* **MICHAEL**.*)*

COUNSELOR SUE. Why do I always think I'm just walking in on something in this cottage?

(They all try to hide their excitement about seeing **MICHAEL**.*)*

COUNSELOR SUE. *(to* **MICHAEL***)* You going to be all right, Allen?

MICHAEL. Absolutely. Thank you for the escort.

COUNSELOR SUE. Let's keep this reunion a short one… after seeing your test scores today you all need to spend more time studying.

*(***COUNSELOR SUE** *gives one last scrutinizing look at the group and then exits. After she is gone…the others gather around* **MICHAEL**.*)*

SANDRA. We were so worried about you.

WENDY. What happened?

ZOOM. Yeah, we were sure you were a goner.

MICHAEL. Well, I thought I was a goner, too. But a miracle happened. I had a visitor.

SANDRA. Your Original came for you?

MICHAEL. My Original's sister came to meet me.

BETTY. Through thick and thin, she's next of kin.

WENDY. Sister? Why didn't your Original come?

MICHAEL. I'll tell you the whole story later.

SANDRA. So are you going home with them?

MICHAEL. In time. Just like the rest of you, I'm going to have to wait it out. But at least I have something to wait for now.

ZOOM. So you're not gonna be harvested?

MICHAEL. Maybe someday, but I don't count on that happening for a long long time.

(*BETTY hugs MICHAEL.*)

BETTY. We've gone from sad, to being real glad.

MICHAEL. Thanks, Betty. But under the circumstances I'm more sad than glad.

(*pause*)

But here's something to make all of us a lot happier...I have proof that Melissa is okay and still out there fighting for our rights.

WENDY. You do?

MICHAEL. My Original's sister came here because she got a call from Counselor "Melissa"...two days ago!

ZOOM. Melissa's a Counselor now?

MICHAEL. Only on the outside, Zoom.

ZOOM. Outside?

MICHAEL. Out there in the real world. The big open cradle of humanity way beyond the confines of these walls. The place where Originals live free. Melissa is now among them. Dancing full of life. Dancing for all of us.

WENDY. She's going to do it. She's going to turn this world upside down.

(*An electronic buzzer is heard.*)

MICHAEL. Come on, I've got my appetite back. I think tonight I could even eat the lousy nutrients the cafeteria serves.

WENDY. You can have mine then...'cause I'm on liquids for awhile. Gonna lose ten more pounds by the end of next week.

(They start to head out.)

SANDRA. Michael, guess what…we're getting a new Copy tomorrow.

BETTY. Fresh flesh!

WENDY. What kind of initiation you gonna give 'em, Michael?

MICHAEL. Me?

ZOOM. Yeah, you're the new number one.

WENDY. Melissa would want you to continue her tradition.

MICHAEL. If that's what she would want, then that's what I will do. I'll think of an appropriate initiation. *(beat)* But one thing's for sure…it won't be "Search the Urge."

(They all laugh at that as they exit. **BETTY** *lags behind for a moment. She speaks directly to the audience.)*

BETTY. The longer we stay here the harder it seems.
Is this someone's nightmare or just our bad dream?
We study and learn and wait for the day
When our Original asks us to come home and stay.

*(***BETTY*** realizes she's alone and then runs off stage to join the others.)*

End of Play

**Also by
Brad Slaight...**

Class Action

High Tide and Sightings

Middle Class

The Road Taken

Second Class

Please visit our website **bakersplays.com** for complete descriptions and licensing information

OTHER TITLES AVAILABLE FROM BAKER'S PLAYS

CLASS ACTION
Brad Slaight

Flexible cast
An evening of twenty-five short scenes and monologues.

Commissioned by the Tony Award winning American Conservatory Theater (A.C.T.) In San Francisco, this play has won critical acclaim for its entertaining yet relevant and realistic portrayal of life at a High School.

The many diverse scenes collectively make up the play. Although each scene stands on its own, there is a common thread - all of the vignettes deal with situations that take place outside the classroom, perhaps the most important experiences that young people deal with while attending High School. The scenes cover a wide variety of contemporary subjects, both serious and light hearted, and audiences of any age can relate to the universal themes. Among the many subjects are: prom night, home work, alcoholism, teen pregnancy, detention, teen idols, peer pressure and class elections. The play's mix of comedy and drama will both entertain and enlighten all in the same evening. Student actors in the original production expressed their appreciation for words, thoughts and ideas that they could relate to. As one student put it, "Finally, a play that speaks the way we do and treats us like human beings with real emotions and feelings." Brad Slaight, a professional Los Angeles-based actor and writer, is also the author of two favorite Baker's Plays one-acts, *Sightings* and *High Tide*.

BAKERSPLAYS.COM

OTHER TITLES AVAILABLE FROM BAKER'S PLAYS

SECOND CLASS
Brad Slaight

4m, 6f / Flexible casting / suggested scenery
full length play runs 90 minutes

Everybody in high school knows that the real learning takes place outside the classroom - in the halls, outside the school before the bell, hangin' out in the parking lot.

This continuation of *Class Action* covers a variety of contemporary subjects, both serious and lighthearted. In too many plays, high school students are presented as angst-ridden teens desperately trying to make it through each day. Yes, there are plenty of obstacles, but as this play shows, there are plenty of good times and lots of laughter, too. The many scenes and monologues have been arranged in a "suggested" order and you may find it necessary to change the order and/or omit some of the scenes depending on your needs.

From the author of *Class Action, Sightings, High Tide, The Road Taken* etc.

BAKERSPLAYS.COM

OTHER TITLES AVAILABLE FROM BAKER'S PLAYS

MIDDLE CLASS
Brad Slaight

10 Students - 4m, 6f / Flexible Cast / Simple Set
Middle Class is a continuation of the popular "class" play cycle written especially for young actors by Brad Slaight. Like the earlier *Class Action* and *Second Class, Middle Class* explores the tribulations of young people while in school. Where the other two plays dealt with high school aged characters, *Middle Class* concerns a group of young people in a modern middle school (junior high). Incorporating an ensemble of players, taking on numerous roles, the play offers insight (often humorous, often poignant) into the issues facing young people during the complex transition from grade school to high school. Such themes as identity, personal relations, status, expectations, and competitiveness are central to the play.

Middle Class was commissioned by the Young Conservatory at the Tony Award winning American Conservatory Theater (A.C.T.) in San Francisco.

BAKERSPLAYS.COM

www.ingramcontent.com/pod-product-compliance
Lightning Source LLC
Chambersburg PA
CBHW071837290426
44109CB00017B/1843